PASSOVER
Before Messiah and After

by

Donna and Mal Broadhurst

Shofar Publications, Inc.
Carol Stream, Illinois

Scripture quotations from the King James Version.
Cover by Caffy Whitney.
Typography by Laura Taggart Dziedzic.

Shofar Publications, Inc.
P.O. Box 88711
Carol Stream, IL 60188

Printed in the United States of America.

Library of Congress Catalog Card Number: 86-63643

ISBN 0-936685-00-X

PREFACE

This is a book for those who want to understand the meaning of Passover and its relation to "Easter" and Communion. It has an in-depth Bible study (chapters 1-9) and a section on post-Biblical history and traditions (chapters 10-14). Three appendices provide pertinent technical data.

The Bible study answers many basic questions, such as:

Why did God command the ancient Hebrews to sacrifice lambs and put the blood on their doors? What did He see when He looked at the passover lambs' blood?

What did the Lord mean when He commanded His people to observe Passover **forever**? Are Christians who have turned to the God of Abraham, Isaac and Jacob to observe Passover?

What did Jesus do with Passover observance when He instituted the bread and wine commemoration of His death?

Why are followers of Jesus pictured in Revelation singing the song of **Moses** and the Lamb?

The section on traditions and history answers other crucial questions:

Why have Christians through the centuries given the annual celebration of Christ's death and resurrection names such as "The Lord's Passover," "Paschaltide," and "The Christian Passover?"

What was "The Paschal Controversy," and how was it settled?

When was "The Christian Passover" renamed "Easter," and why?

Why are many twentieth-century Christians more familiar with the Easter Bunny than with the Pascal Lamb?

What is the "blood libel" Christians leveled at Jews for centuries during Passover?

How do Jewish people celebrate Passover today? What is the Haggadah?

Passover Before Messiah and After brings out many interesting and thought-provoking facts. For example:

Passover and the Feast of Unleavened Bread are technically two distinct institutions with different commemorative emphases.

Gentiles were included in God's Holy Nation at its formation in the Exodus, and observed Passover with the Children of Israel throughout Biblical history.

A great multitude of Jews applied a Messianic Passover Psalm to Jesus as He entered Jerusalem for His last Passover.

Jesus, who the Apostle Paul called "the Firstfruits of them that sleep," rose from the dead on Firstfruits Sunday—a little-emphasized observance the Lord designated in Leviticus for every Sunday of every Passover week.

For the reader's convenience, all passages of the Law and the New Testament which speak explicitly of Passover are completely written out in the text. So are many other related verses. All other Scripture references are noted in parentheses. It is well worth the time and effort to look up all the Scripture verses and read them in their context.

As the reader new to this subject will discover, Passover does not have to do with a single theme of Scripture which can be examined in isolation. God's revelation is a unity—a tapestry of countless threads interwoven in an intricate and complex design. What seems to be the "thread of Passover" beginning with such simplicity in the ritual of Exodus 12 soon becomes "lost" in the whole of Scripture's message of redemption.

Similarly, Passover is interwoven with the whole fabric of post-Biblical history. It becomes impossible to follow every thread. In a book like this, one must settle for a few thoughts which are merely suggestive of Passover's infinite and eternal truths. There is no way to exhaust this subject.

CONTENTS

PASSOVER BEFORE MESSIAH
IN THE BIBLE

PASSOVER AFTER MESSIAH
IN THE BIBLE

Contents

PASSOVER IN THE POST-BIBLICAL RELIGIOUS TRADITIONS

In Memory Of
Ray and Naomi Knapp

1

THE LORD'S PASSOVER

They shall take to them every man a lamb. . . a lamb for an house. . . without blemish, a male of the first year. . . and the whole assembly of the congregation of Israel shall kill it in the evening. And they shall take of the blood, and strike it on the two side posts and on the upper door post of the houses, wherein they shall eat it. . . it is the LORD's passover.

(Exodus 12:3-11)

When the Lord delivered Israel from bondage in ancient Egypt, He did so with an awesome display of His sovereign power. With many signs and miracles, He demonstrated to Israel and Egypt alike that He was the Lord.

The Bible's narrative of this deliverance (Exodus 1-15) is vivid: Hebrew slaves toiling as brickmakers and builders of Pharaoh's treasure cities, a baby in a basket floating amidst river reeds until found by Pharaoh's daughter, a bush that burned but was not consumed, Moses and Aaron in Pharaoh's palace confronting magicians with a rod that became a serpent, rivers turned to blood, plagues of swarming flies and locusts, infestations of lice and frogs, boils covering man and beast, hail and fire raining from heaven, darkness thick enough to be felt, a terrifying death plague that selectively touched only firstborn men and animals, hundreds of thousands of people with their worldly goods, animal herds and Egyptian treasures leaving Goshen in a mass exodus, the Red Sea parting to let the children of Israel cross on dry ground, the walls of water crashing down upon the pursuing Egyptian army with their horses and chariots, Israel's thousands singing together the triumphant song of Moses.

9

God gave Israel a unique experience. Not before, and not since, has He provided temporal deliverance with such a spectacular display of His sovereignty.

Out of all the memorable events of the Exodus, the Lord designated one to be remembered in a special way: His deliverance of Israel from the tenth plague, the death of the firstborn, by the sacrifice of the passover lamb. That event was so important in God's eyes that He **commanded** the people to remember it forever; to perpetuate it in all their generations. The salvation of the firstborn by the passover is recounted in Exodus 11 and 12.

The Tenth Plague and Egypt

The plagues God sent on Egypt were not acts of angry vindictiveness or mere retribution upon Egypt for oppressing the Hebrews, although punishment was involved. They were part of the Sovereign Lord's plan to teach Egypt as well as Israel that He was the Lord (Ex. 7:5,17).

The Lord is loving, patient and fair, as well as powerful and just. As He said to Pharaoh, if all He'd wanted to do was wipe Pharaoh and his people off the face of the earth, He would have done just that at the beginning. But He'd sent the lesser plagues to give the Egyptians a chance to know Him and His glory, too (Ex. 9:14-17).

The plagues instructed Egypt about God. They showed that He was a God of power and might (Ex. 7:3; 10:1, 11:9), that there was no god like the Lord (Ex. 8:10), that there was none other like Him in the earth (Ex. 9:14), that the earth was His (Ex. 9:29), and that He was in the midst of the land intervening in nature and the affairs of men (Ex. 8:22-23).

The plagues could have helped Pharaoh humble himself before the Lord (Ex. 10:3). But instead Pharaoh stubbornly refused to acknowledge the Lord and submit to Him. It's true God hardened Pharaoh's heart (Ex. 9:12), but Pharaoh also hardened his own heart (Ex. 8:32). As Pharaoh refused to submit voluntarily to the Lord, the plagues increased in severity, convincing and compelling him to acknowledge the Lord and obey His word to let His people go (Ex. 3:19-20; 6:1).

The plagues did change Pharaoh's knowledge of, and attitude about, the Lord. Pharaoh, who had at first said, "Who is the Lord, that I should obey his voice and let Israel go? I know not the Lord" (Ex. 5:2), came to the point where he said he had been wrong about the Lord: "I have sinned this time: the Lord is righteous, and I and my people are wicked" (Ex. 9:27). Later he even asked forgiveness (Ex. 10:17) and asked Moses to bless him (Ex. 12:32).

Other Egyptians changed their attitudes, too. The initially-smug magicians, who had duplicated the first two plagues but could do no more, acknowledged, "This is the finger of God" (Ex. 8:19). Pharaoh's servants recognized that Egypt was being destroyed because of Pharaoh's refusal to let the Israelites go (Ex. 10:7). By the seventh plague of hail, there were Egyptians who "feared the word of the Lord" and took the precautions God said to take in order to escape death from the hail (Ex. 9:20). The people of Egypt with Pharaoh's servants came to think favorably of the Israelites. They considered Moses a great man (Ex. 11:3).

But Pharaoh, in that he encountered the Lord in the first nine plagues and learned much about Him, yet refused to submit to Him (Ex. 9:17, 30), came under God's punishment. The plagues that could have led him to worship God became judgments upon him and his land (Ex. 6:1; 7:4).

Because he didn't bow to the Lord voluntarily, God made Pharaoh submit involuntarily by bringing greater power against him in the final plagues (Ex. 9:14).

The tenth plague was most severe of all; it forced Pharaoh to obey the Lord and let His people go:

> And the LORD said unto Moses, Yet will I bring one
> plague more upon Pharaoh, and upon Egypt; after-

*wards he will let you go hence: when he shall let you
go, he shall surely thrust you out hence altogether.*

*And Moses said, Thus saith the LORD About midnight
will I go out into the midst of Egypt: and all the
firstborn in the land of Egypt shall die, from the
firstborn of Pharaoh that sitteth upon his throne,
even unto the firstborn of the maidservant that is
behind the mill; and all the firstborn of beasts.*

*And there shall be a great cry throughout all the
land of Egypt, such as there was none like it, nor
shall be any like it any more.*

*But against any of the children of Israel shall not a
dog move his tongue, against man or beast: that ye
may know how that the LORD doth put a difference
between the Egyptians and Israel. (Exodus 11:1, 4-7)*

*For I will pass through the land of Egypt this night,
and will smite all the firstborn in the land of Egypt,
both man and beast; and against all the gods of
Egypt I will execute judgment: I am the LORD.*
(Exodus 12:12)

When it came, the tenth plague was devestating. It resulted
in the Egyptians thrusting Israel from their land:

*And it came to pass that at midnight the LORD smote
all the firstborn in the land of Egypt, from the
firstborn of Pharaoh that sat on his throne unto the
firstborn of the captive that was in the dungeon; and
all the firstborn of cattle.*

*And Pharaoh rose up in the night, he, and all his
servants, and all the Egyptians; and there was a
great cry in Egypt, for there was not a house where
there was not one dead.*

*And he called for Moses and Aaron by night, and
said, Rise up, and get you forth from among my
people, both ye and the children of Israel; and go,*

serve the LORD as ye have said. Also take your flocks and your herds, as ye have said, and be gone; and bless me also.

And the Egyptians were urgent upon the people, that they might send them out of the land in haste; for they said, We be all dead men.

And the people took their dough before it was leavened, their kneading troughs being bound up in their clothes upon their shoulders.

And the children of Israel did according to the word of Moses; and they borrowed of the Egyptians jewels of silver, and jewels of gold, and raiment: and the LORD gave the people favour in the sight of the Egyptians, so that they lent unto them such things as they required. And they spoiled the Egyptians. . .

It is a night to be much observed unto the LORD for bringing them out from the land of Egypt: this is that night of the LORD to be observed of all the children of Israel in their generations.

(Exodus 12:29-36,42)

Scripture doesn't state whether or not the Egyptians were told of God's provision of the sacrifice lamb; whether or not they had the same chance as Israel to escape the tenth plague. If they did know about the passover sacrifice, those Egyptians who had come to fear the word of the Lord (Ex. 9:20) would undoubtedly have heeded God's warning about the tenth plague just as they had heeded His warning about the hail. It seems that some Egyptians and Hebrews lived together in the same houses (Ex. 3:22); perhaps some of those escaped the plague with their Hebrew housemates.

At any rate, whether or not any escaped the tenth plague, it seems likely that some Egyptians were part of the "mixed multitude" who left Egypt with Israel in the exodus (Ex. 12:38). A certain "Bithiah, Pharaoh's daughter" is listed in the genealogies of Judah from about that period (I Chron. 4:18). God gave instructions concerning the inclusion of these and future "strangers" in passover observance (Ex. 12:43-49; Nu. 9:14).

The Tenth Plague and Israel

God sent the plagues to instruct Israel as well as Egypt. Because of them, **Egypt** would know He was the Lord (Ex. 7:5, 17); because of them, **Israel** would know He was the Lord (Ex. 10:2).

God had revealed Himself to Abraham, Isaac and Jacob only as *El Shaddai*, God Almighty. But to Moses He made Himself known as "I AM" (Ex. 3:14) and *Yehovah*, the Lord, who established covenant with Israel (Ex. 6:2-6). God told Moses Israel would see His wonders and would know He was the Lord their God (Ex. 6:7) who established covenant with them (Ex. 6:4) and gave the land of Canaan to them (Ex. 6:4). They would know He had redeemed them (Ex. 6:6). By those great judgments Israel would know that the Lord (not they themselves, or coincidence) had brought them out from the bondage of the Egyptians (Ex. 6:6-7). They would know He took them for a people (initiating the relationship) and became their God (Ex. 6:7). And they would know He brought them into the land He gave them as a heritage (Ex. 6:8). They would know He was the Lord (Ex. 10:2).

God's supernatural plagues would confirm and reinforce to Israel that He was El Shaddai—God Almighty, Sovereign over nature, over men, and over the gods men created. The plagues would teach them that He, Yehovah their God, made a distinction between them and Egypt (Ex. 8:22-23).

In "distinguishing between Egypt and Israel," God shielded Israel from most, if not all of the harm from the plagues. Of the first nine, it's definitely stated that Israel had no swarming flies (Ex. 8:22), lost none of their livestock to the disease plague (Ex. 9:6), had no hail in Goshen (Ex. 9:26) and had light in their dwellings during the plague of darkness (Ex. 10:23).

The Hebrews apparently did have to contend with the darkness outside their houses. The Bible seems clear that the hail and locusts destroyed every plant in all of Egypt, but Israel would be leaving in a short time, so the destruction of the future food sources would not affect them.

Israel had to do nothing to be spared from the first nine plagues. But the tenth plague, the death of the firstborn, was upon Israel in the same way it was upon Egypt unless they heeded God's warning and made the required sacrifice. Without the sacrifice, the Hebrews' firstborn as well as the Egyptians' would be slain.

Although the Lord had foretold that none of the children of Israel would perish in the death plague (Ex. 11:7), the firstborn in fact were spared only as each family sacrificed the lamb and put its blood on their doors. "When I see the blood, I will pass over you, and the plague shall not be upon you to destroy you when I smite the land of Egypt," the Lord had said (Ex. 12:12-13). If there had been a Hebrew household without the lamb's blood upon its door, the firstborn within would have perished with the Egyptians.

What was this judgment on all the people? Why was Israel under it as well as Egypt? If they did not know at the time, they would learn more in days to come as God unfolded His revelation of eternal truth to them. For the time being, all they needed to know was to obey. God instructed them how to be spared His judgment by a blood sacrifice.

The Passover Sacrifice

The Lord gave explicit instructions about the sacrifice which would save Israel from the death of their firstborn. Each family was to sacrifice a perfect lamb; the entire congregation of Israel was to sacrifice the lambs on the evening of the 14th of that month (Abib, later called Nisan):

> *And the LORD spake unto Moses and Aaron in the*
> *land of Egypt, saying, This month shall be unto you*
> *the beginning of months: it shall be the first month*
> *of the year to you.*
>
> *Speak ye unto all the congregation of Israel saying,*
> *In the tenth day of this month they shall take to*
> *them every man a lamb, according to the house of*
> *their fathers, a lamb for an house: and if the*
> *household be too little for the lamb, let him and his*
> *neighbour next unto his house take it according to*
> *the number of the souls; every man according to his*
> *eating shall make your count for the lamb.*
>
> *Your lamb shall be without blemish, a male of the*
> *first year: ye shall take it out from the sheep, or*
> *from the goats: and ye shall keep it up until the*
> *fourteenth day of the same month: and the whole*
> *assembly of the congregation of Israel shall kill it in*
> *the evening.*   *(Ex. 12:1-6)*

Each family was to mark its dwelling in a certain way with
the blood of the sacrificed lamb:

> *And they shall take of the blood, and strike it on the*
> *two side posts and on the upper door post of the*
> *houses, wherein they shall eat it.*   *(Ex. 12:7).*

They were to prepare the lamb according to detailed instructions, and eat it ritually with unleavened bread and bitter herbs.

> *And they shall eat the flesh in that night, roast with*
> *fire, and unleavened bread; and with bitter herbs*
> *they shall eat it.*
>
> *Eat not of it raw, nor sodden at all with water, but*
> *roast it with fire, his head with his legs, and with*
> *the purtenance thereof. And ye shall let nothing of it*
> *remain until the morning; and that which*

remaineth of it until the morning ye shall burn
with fire.

And thus shall ye eat it; with your loins girded, and
your shoes on your feet, and your staff in your
hand; and ye shall eat it in haste: It is the LORD'S
passover. *(Ex. 12:8-11).*

"The Lord's Passover" sacrifice would hold back the Lord's hand of judgment:

For I will pass through the land of Egypt this night,
and will smite all the firstborn in the land of Egypt,
both man and beast; and against all the gods of
Egypt I will execute judgment: I am the LORD.

And the blood shall be to you for a token upon the
houses where you are: and when I see the blood, I
will pass over you, and the plague shall not be upon
you to destroy you, when I smite the land of Egypt.
(Ex. 12:12-13)

God commanded that the day of His redemption by the passover sacrifice be celebrated perpetually:

And this day shall be unto you for a memorial;
and ye shall keep it a feast to the LORD throughout
your generations; ye shall keep it a feast by an
ordinance for ever. *(Ex. 12:14)*

. . .

Then Moses called for all the elders of Israel, and
said unto them, Draw out and take you a lamb
according to your families, and kill the passover.

And ye shall take a bunch of hyssop, and dip it in
the blood that is in the bason, and strike the lintel
and the two side posts with the blood that is in the
bason; and none of you shall go out at the door of
his house until morning. For the LORD will pass
through to smite the Egyptians; and when he seeth
the blood upon the lintel, and on the two side posts,

> *the LORD will pass over the door, and will not*
> *suffer the destroyer to come in unto your houses*
> *to smite you.*
>
> *And ye shall observe this thing for an ordinance to*
> *thee and to thy sons for ever.*   *(Ex. 12:21-24)*

Israel was to tell their children in all the days to come about the redemption God provided in Egypt:

> *And it shall come to pass, when ye be come to the*
> *land which the LORD will give you, according as he*
> *hath promised, that ye shall keep this service. And it*
> *shall come to pass, when your children say unto*
> *you, What mean ye by this service? That ye shall*
> *say, It is the sacrifice of the LORD'S Passover, who*
> *passed over the houses of the children of Israel in*
> *Egypt, when he smote the Egyptians, and delivered*
> *our houses. And the people bowed the head and*
> *worshipped.*   *(Ex. 12:25-28)*

The Children of Israel obeyed the Lord's word through Moses and Aaron. The supernatural plague that selectively touched the firstborn did not destroy any of them. It finally convinced Pharaoh that he must submit to the Lord's sovereignty and let His people go as He had demanded:

> *And it came to pass that at midnight the LORD smote*
> *all the firstborn in the land of Egypt, from the*
> *firstborn of Pharaoh that sat on his throne unto the*
> *firstborn of the captive that was in the dungeon; and*
> *all the firstborn of cattle.*
>
> *And Pharaoh rose up in the night, he, and all his*
> *servants, and all the Egyptians; and there was a*
> *great cry in Egypt, for there was not a house where*
> *there was not one dead.*
>
> *And he called for Moses and Aaron by night, and*
> *said, Rise up, and get you forth from among my*

*people, both ye and the children of Israel; and go,
serve the LORD, as ye have said.   (Ex. 12:28-31)*

Rules About the Lamb and Sacrificing It

The passover lamb had to be perfect—no flaws. It had to be a young male, less than a year old. It could be a lamb from the sheep or from the goats (Ex. 12:5).

God gave the people detailed instructions for sacrificing the passover that night in Egypt. There were rules about the date and time of the sacrifice, about putting its blood on the doors, and about how to cook and eat it.

It was the beginning of a month (Abib, later called Nisan) when God gave Moses and Aaron His word about the passover sacrifice (Ex. 12:1). He said that on the tenth day of that month each family was to select a perfect young male lamb from its sheep or goats (Ex. 12:5). This lamb would be eaten after it was sacrificed, and all of it had to be eaten. So if a household were a small one, it was to combine with a nearby neighbor family to sacrifice and eat the lamb. (Ex. 12:4, 10). The lamb was to be kept in a special place from the tenth day until the fourteenth when it was to be killed in the evening (Ex. 12:6).

The sacrifice of the lambs was not a private matter for each household, but a community ceremony. The entire nation in assembly was to kill the lambs in a unified act (Ex. 12:3-6, 21).

Each family had to put their lamb's blood on their door. The blood had to be struck on with a bunch of hyssop (an Egyptian plant) over the top of the door and on each sidepost (Ex. 12:7, 22).

The lamb had to be roasted; it couldn't be eaten raw or boiled. It had to be roasted whole, including head, legs and inner parts. All of it had to be eaten before morning, or be burned (Ex. 12:8-10). The lamb was to be eaten with bitter herbs and unleavened bread (Ex. 12:8). It had to be eaten in haste. The family was to be dressed in travel clothes, ready to leave Egypt quickly (Ex. 12:11).

The people were to stay inside their houses all night, not going out at all. For the Lord would pass through the land in the middle of the night to destroy the firstborn. When He saw the blood on a house, He would pass over that house while the family inside was eating the passover (Ex. 12:22-23).

The Lamb Was Central

The writer of Hebrews sums up passover in one verse: "Through faith he [Moses] kept the passover and the sprinkling of blood, lest He that destroyed the firstborn should touch them." (Hebrews 11:28).

While Israel's deliverance from Egyptian slavery was accomplished by all the plagues and miracles God did in the land, their deliverance from the Lord's tenth-plague judgment was accomplished by the blood of the sacrificed lamb. God called the lamb sacrifice "The Lord's Passover" (Ex. 12:11).

The sacrifice was named "The Lord's **Passover**" (*pesach*, in Hebrew) because it would cause the Lord to "pass over" (*pasach*) the family with the sacrifice's blood on their door. Perhaps it was called "The **Lord's** Passover" because it was He Himself who destroyed or passed over the firstborn in each home. Possibly it was called "The **Lord's** because it was for Him. He had a right to the offering. The family owed it to Him in exchange for the life of the firstborn which He had a right to take by death in His just and fair judgment. Or perhaps it was called The **Lord's** because He had initiated and provided the sacrifice for the people as their way of escape. In a prophetic sense, The Lord's Passover had ultimate meaning that would unfold as God added revelation to revelation.

2

A FEAST FOREVER

And this day shall be unto you for a memorial; and ye shall keep it a feast to the LORD throughout your generations; ye shall keep it a feast by an ordinance for ever.
(Exodus 12:14)

As the Lord spoke to Moses and Aaron about the Passover, He made it clear that it was of utmost significance. "This month shall be unto you the beginning of months," the Lord declared. "It shall be the first month of the year to you" (Ex. 12:1). Every aspect of their lives as His people—daily routine and religious ceremony, would date from the Passover and relate to it.

The awesome night in which God delivered Israel from His own judgment was to be commemorated forever, in all Israel's generations. It was to be commemorated by the ceremonial passover sacrifice on the 14th of Nisan, and by a ceremonial feast at which the lamb was eaten:

> *And this day shall be unto you for a memorial; and ye shall keep it a feast to the LORD throughout your generations; ye shall keep it a feast by an ordinance for ever. (Ex. 12:14)*
>
> *And ye shall observe this thing for an ordinance to thee and to thy sons for ever. And it shall come to pass, when ye be come to the land which the LORD will give you, according as he hath promised, that ye shall keep this service. And it shall come to pass when your children shall say unto you. What mean ye by this service? That ye shall say, It is the sacrifice of the LORD's passover, who passed over the houses of the children of Israel in Egypt, when he smote the Egyptians, and delivered our houses. (Ex. 12:24-27)*

21

It is a night to be much observed unto the LORD for bringing them out from the land of Egypt: this is that night of the LORD to be observed of all the children of Israel in their generations. (Ex. 12:42)

The Lord did not say the firstborn would be in danger of a death plague every year, but He commanded Israel to sacrifice passover lambs every year on the anniversary of the tenth plague and original passover sacrifice in Egypt.

Certainly the Israelites wondered about the meaning of the annual sacrifice. From what judgment had **they,** God's chosen people, needed salvation in Egypt? What kind of judgment extended through all their generations, through all their growth, development and increasing knowledge? Regarding what did the Holy One need placation?

Israel did have the lessons about the animals God slew to cover Adam and Eve in Eden (Gen. 3:21), about Abel's acceptable sacrifice of the firstlings of his flock (Gen. 4:2-7), and about Noah's sacrifice animals (Gen. 7:2-3, 8; 8:20-21). They knew about God ordering the death of Abraham's and Sarah's firstborn, the son of promise, and then Himself providing the lamb offering in Isaac's place (Gen. 22:1-14). But what did it all mean? Why did there need to be continuing passover sacrifice? Why must life be given in exchange for life?

After the passover sacrifice, God instituted other animal sacrifices. God said that through blood sacrifice atonement for sin would be made and a person's sins forgiven. (Lev. 4:32-35 and 10:17). He said, "For the life of the flesh is in the blood; and I have given it to you upon the altar to make atonement for your souls; for it is the blood that maketh atonement by reason of the life" (Lev. 17:11).

It still was not clear. What spiritual exchange in the high heavens was involved in the principle of blood atonement? What mysterious transaction between God and man? Israel had not yet received the word of the Prophets, much less the revelation of "The Lamb slain from the foundation of the world" (Rev. 13:8; Jn. 1:29). They could only wonder and obey.

There were many details to obey in the Passover observance. In addition to the regulations already given, God gave further instructions about the ceremony of sacrifice and the ceremony of eating the passover lamb.

These regulations concerned "strangers" who wished to observe the Passover, observing Passover only at one place of worship designated by God, and the second-month Passover for the ritually unclean. Also the consecration of the firstborn and the seven days of eating unleavened bread with additional sacrifices.

Passover Rules For "Strangers"

From the beginning, the congregation of Israel included not only blood descendants of Abraham, Isaac and Jacob, but also people from other tribes of earth who had drawn near to the God of Israel.

A "mixed multitude" left Egypt with the children of Israel (Ex. 12:38) and were in unity with the blood descendants of Israel. In speaking about the "congregation of Israel" in Exodus 12:19, God said that it included "strangers" as well as "those born in the land." These were one congregation of His people. If any broke His laws, he would be cut off from the congregation; he would be cut off from being one of God's people— whether a stranger or one born in the land as a blood descendant of Israel. Any uncircumcised, for example, was cut off from being one of God's people (Gen. 17:14).

The rule for the stranger who wished to keep the Passover was essentially that he become an Israelite in all respects except his blood lineage, which of course he could not change. He was to be circumcised, receiving the permanent mark of one in covenant with the Lord, and he was to live as the Israelites, **keeping** covenant with God by obeying all His rules. He was then no longer a stranger, for a stranger could not eat the

Passover. He became, and remained, one of the people of God just as the descendants of Abraham, Isaac, and Jacob became and remained the people of God—by circumcision and obedience to His laws:

> *And the LORD said unto Moses and Aaron, This is*
> *the ordinance of the passover: There shall no*
> *stranger eat thereof: But every man's servant that is*
> *bought for money, when thou hast circumcised him,*
> *then shall he eat thereof. A foreigner and an hired*
> *servant shall not eat thereof. In one house shall it be*
> *eaten; thou shalt not carry forth ought of the flesh*
> *abroad out of the house; neither shall ye break a*
> *bone thereof. All the congregration of Israel shall*
> *keep it. And when a stranger shall sojourn with*
> *thee, and will keep the passover to the LORD, let all*
> *his males be circumcised, and then let him come*
> *near and keep it; and he shall be as one that is born*
> *in the land: for no uncircumcised person shall eat*
> *thereof. One law shall be to him that is homeborn,*
> *and unto the stranger that sojourneth among you.*
> *(Ex. 12:43-49)*

In the midst of His rules concerning strangers observing the Passover, God put the two rules about no bone of the lamb being broken and none of its meat being carried from the house. He had already decreed that the lambs had to be slain in one community act and roasted whole. Israel's sons could not separate themselves from the people of other blood lineage to observe the Passover. They couldn't send the servants off with a leg of lamb to observe Passover while they celebrated without them in the house. The people who observed Passover had to do so as one community, one people, one "family of God," sharing together the blessings and benefits symbolized by Passover:

> *And if a stranger shall sojourn among you, and will*
> *keep the passover unto the LORD; according to the*

ordinance of the passover, and according to the manner thereof, so shall he do: ye shall have one ordinance, both for the stranger, and for him that was born in the land. (Nu. 9:14)

And if a stranger sojourn with thee in your land, ye shall not vex him. But the stranger that dwelleth with you shall be unto you as one born among you, and thou shalt love him as thyself; for ye were strangers in the land of Egypt: I am the LORD your God. (Lev. 19:33-34)

The Lord did not give His revelation and laws to the nations. He did not establish covenant with other nations as He did with Israel. But if anyone heard about Him and wanted to worship the God of Israel, he could do so in community with Israel, obeying the same laws and sharing the same destiny. Even uninvited by Israel, strangers could draw near to the Lord if they wished, and Israel could not forbid them. Such people had to be circumcised and take upon themselves the whole law of God, as did Israel. For the strangers, as for Israel, Passover was not only an opportunity, but an obligation. They **had** to observe it if they wanted to worship the Lord.

Throughout Israel's history as a nation, the congregation of God's people was a "mixed multitude" of Israel's blood descendants and strangers who had drawn near to God. Sometimes people from other nations came to the Lord as individuals— for example, Ruth and Rahab. Sometimes great numbers came to Him during momentous events. In the beginning, a multitude left Egypt with Israel in the Exodus. Those people of this multitude who were circumcised and consented to obey the God of Israel, although not born of Jacob's lineage, were nevertheless part of the people God formed into His holy nation. Later, in Esther's day, many Persians "became Jews" and were added to the holy nation (Esther 8:17).

The records of revival under Hezekiah and Ezra state that

people from other nations who turned to the Lord, as well as those from Israel who turned back to the Lord, observed Passover together (II Chron. 30:25 and Ezra 6:21).

Strangers who were circumcised and kept the Law intermarried with the descendants of Israel. Neither Israel, nor any other tribe of earth, has had a "pure racial lineage;" there is no such thing; mankind is one. Israel was the holy nation only as it kept covenant with God and thereby maintained pure religious ceremonies and the pure lifestye of God's Law. Jacob's descendants as well as strangers were cut off from the holy nation when they disobeyed.

The One Place of Worship

When Moses repeated the words of God just before the people were about to enter the promised land, he said that from that time onward the Tabernacle was the place where the congregated nation was to sacrifice the passover lambs and eat the ceremonial meal. The Tabernacle, wherever it was pitched, was the place in which the Lord "put His name:"

> *Thou shalt therefore sacrifice the passover unto the LORD thy God, of the flock and the herd, in the place which the LORD shall choose to place his name there... Thou mayest not sacrifice the passover within any of thy gates, which the LORD thy God giveth thee: but at the place which the LORD thy God shall choose to place his name in, there thou shalt sacrifice the passover at even, at the going down of the sun, at the season that thou camest forth out of Egypt. And thou shalt roast and eat it in the place which the LORD thy God shall choose: and thou shalt turn in the morning, and go unto thy tents.*
> *(Deut. 16:2,5-7)*

The Second-Month Passover

Certain conditions, such as being ritually unclean from contact with a dead body (Lev. 22:4-7; Nu. 5:2) or being away on a journey in a distant place, might render a person ineligible to observe Passover at the designated time and place. For such cases, God instructed those involved to observe Passover on the 14th of the second month (Nu. 9:6-10). It was to be observed according to "all the ordinances" of the regular Passover (Nu. 9:11).

The Lord repeated some of the most important instructions: the passover lamb must be slain at evening, it must be eaten with unleavened bread and bitter herbs, it must be consumed before morning, and it must remain whole—not a bone could be broken. (Nu. 9:11-12) Here God gave His most serious word about the consequences of not observing Passover: the person who refused to keep the Passover was to be cut off from the people of God because he "brought not the offering of the Lord." That person "shall bear his sin." (Nu. 9:13)

Consecration of the Firstborn

Since the Lord had spared the firstborn of Israel in Egypt (and continued to spare them, it could be said), They belonged to Him—both animals and men. They were consecrated to Him. God gave rules that firstborn animals consecrated to Him had to be sacrificed. Firstborn men, He said, were to be "redeemed"—bought back with a price given in exchange for their lives being spent in Tabernacle service:

> And the LORD spake unto Moses saying, Sanctify unto me all the firstborn, whatsoever openeth the womb among the children of Israel, both of man and of beast: it is mine. (Ex. 13:1-2)

> And it shall be when the LORD shall bring thee into the land of the Canaanites, as he sware unto thee and to thy fathers, and shall give it thee, that thou shalt set apart unto the LORD all that openeth the matrix, and every firstling that cometh of a beast which thou hast; the males shall be the LORD's. (Ex. 13:11-12)

> *And every firstling of an ass thou shalt redeem with
> a lamb: and if thou wilt not redeem it, then thou
> shalt break his neck: and all the firstborn of man
> among thy children shalt thou redeem. And it shall
> be when thy son asketh thee in time to come, saying,
> What is this? that thou shalt say unto him, By
> strength of hand the LORD brought us out from
> Egypt, from the house of bondage: And it came to
> pass, when Pharaoh would hardly let us go, that the
> LORD slew all the firstborn of man, and the firstborn
> of beast: therefore I sacrifice to the LORD all that
> openeth the matrix, being males; but all the firstborn
> of my children I redeem. And it shall be for a token
> upon thine hand, and for frontlets between thine
> eyes: for by strength of hand the LORD brought us
> forth out of Egypt. (Ex. 13:1-2, 13-16)*

> *All the firstborn of thy sons thou shalt redeem. And
> none shall appear before me empty. (Ex. 34:19-20)*

The firstborn were redeemed with money. Numbers 3:46-51 and Leviticus 27 give an idea of the amount involved in redeeming a man.

Later God commanded that the tribe of Levi be set aside to Him to spend their lives serving Him in the Tabernacle. The Levites became the Lord's in place of the firstborn (Nu. 3:12, 41, 45; 8:13-19).

God called the nation of Israel **His** son, **His** firstborn.

> *And the LORD said unto Moses... thou shalt say unto
> Pharaoh, Thus saith the LORD, Israel is my son, even
> my firstborn. And I say unto thee, Let my son go,
> that he may serve me: and if thou refuse to let him
> go, behold, I will slay thy son, even thy firstborn.
> (Ex. 4:21-23)*

The Seven Days of Unleavened Bread

The ceremony of **sacrificing** the passover lambs took place on the 14th Nisan in the evening as the sun was setting—at the ending of one day and beginning of a new day. (In Hebrew thinking, a new day began at sunset, based on the words "and the evening and the morning were the first day" (Gen 1:5). The ceremony of sacrifice on the 14th spoke of the redemption of the firstborn from the death judgment.

The ceremony of **eating** the passover lambs took place well into the night (dated as the next day) after several hours of roasting the lambs whole. The eating of the passover thus fell on the 15th Nisan which had begun at sunset just after the lambs were slain. The lambs had to be eaten with bitter herbs and unleavened bread; they had to be consumed before dawn that day. The 15th Nisan on which the Passover was eaten, was the first of seven in which unleavened bread had to be eaten. The observance of eating unleavened bread was technically separate from the passover ceremony. While the passover ceremony commemorated redemption from God's own judgment; the eating of unleavened bread commemorated deliverance from Egypt.

Two passages show that Passover and the Feast of Unleavened Bread were two distinct institutions although interrelated:

> *In the fourteenth day of the first month at even is the LORD's passover. And on the fifteenth day of the same month is the feast of unleavened bread unto the LORD: seven days ye must eat unleavened bread. (Lev. 23:5-6)*

> *And the fourteenth day of the first month is the passover of the LORD. And in the fifteenth day of this month is the feast: seven days shall unleavened bread be eaten. (Nu. 28:16-17)*

No Leaven: Not only did the people have to eat unleavened bread for seven days, they had to remove all leaven from their living quarters. Israelites were to tell their children that not eating leaven was symbolic of God's bringing them out of

Egypt. God said any person who ate leaven during the commemoration was to be cut off from His people:

> *Seven days shall ye eat unleavened bread; even the first day ye shall put away leaven out of your houses: for whosoever eateth leavened bread from the first day until the seventh day, that soul shall be cut off from Israel. . . And ye shall observe the feast of unleavened bread; for in this selfsame day have I brought your armies out of the land of Egypt: therefore shall ye observe this day in your generations by an ordinance for ever. In the first month, on the fourteenth day of the month at even, ye shall eat unleavened bread, until the one and twentieth day of the month at even. Seven days shall there be no leaven found in your houses: for whosoever eateth that which is leavened, even that soul shall be cut off from the congregation of Israel, whether he be a stranger, or born in the land. Ye shall eat nothing leavened; in all your habitations shall ye eat unleavened bread. (Ex. 12:15-20)*

> *And Moses said unto the people, Remember this day, in which ye came out from Egypt, out of the house of bondage; for by strength of hand the LORD brought you out from this place: there shall no leavened bread be eaten. This day came ye out in the month Abib. And it shall be when the LORD shall bring thee into the land of the Canaanites, and the Hittities, and the Amorites, and the Hivites, and the Jebusites, which he sware unto thy fathers to give thee, a land flowing with milk and honey, that thou shalt keep this service in this month. Seven days thou shalt eat unleavened bread. . . Unleavened bread shall be eaten seven days; and there shall no leavened bread be seen with thee, neither shall there be leaven seen with thee in all thy quarters. And thou shalt shew thy son in that day, saying, This is done because of*

> *that which the LORD did unto me when I came forth*
> *out of Egypt. And it shall be for a sign unto thee*
> *upon thine hand, and for a memorial between thine*
> *eyes, that the LORD's law may be in thy mouth: for*
> *with a strong hand hath the LORD brought thee out*
> *of Egypt. Thou shall therefore keep this ordinance in*
> *his season from year to year. (Ex. 13:3-10)*

The command to eat unleavened bread with the passover sacrifice and for the duration of seven days is repeated several times:

> *Thou shalt keep the feast of unleavened bread: thou*
> *shalt eat unleavened bread seven days, as I*
> *commanded thee, in the time appointed of the month*
> *Abib; for in it thou camest out from Egypt . . . Thou*
> *shalt not offer the blood of my sacrifice with*
> *leavened bread; neither shall the fat of my sacrifice*
> *remain until the morning." (Ex. 23:14,18)*

> *The feast of unleavened bread shalt thou keep. Seven*
> *days thou shalt eat unleavened bread, as I*
> *commanded thee, in the time of the month Abib:*
> *for in the month Abib thou camest out from Egypt.*
> *(Ex. 34:18)*

> *And on the fifteenth day of the same month is the*
> *feast of unleavened bread unto the LORD: seven days*
> *ye must eat unleavened bread. (Lev. 23:6)*

> *And in the fifteenth day of this month is the feast:*
> *seven days shall unleavened bread be eaten.*
> *(Nu. 28:17)*

> *Thou shalt eat no leavened bread with it [the*
> *Passover]; seven days shalt thou eat unleavened*
> *bread therewith, even the bread of affliction; for thou*
> *camest forth out of the land of Egypt in haste: that*
> *thou mayest remember the day when thou camest*
> *forth out of the land of Egypt all the days of thy life.*

> *And there shall be no leavened bread seen with thee
> in all thy coast seven days. (Deut. 16:3-4)*

Convocations: On the first and seventh days of the week
of eating unleavened bread there was to be a convocation of
all the people. They were to do "no work" on those days save
that necessary for observing the feast days:

> *And in the first day there shall be an holy
> convocation, and in the seventh day there shall be
> an holy convocation to you; no manner of work
> shall be done in them, save that which every man
> must eat, that only may be done of you. (Ex. 12:16)*
>
> *. . . and in the seventh day shall be a feast unto the
> LORD. (Ex. 13:6)*
>
> *In the first day ye shall have a holy convocation: ye
> shall do no servile work therein. . . in the seventh
> day is a holy convocation: ye shall do no servile
> work therein. (Lev. 23:7-8)*
>
> *In the first day shall be an holy convocation; ye
> shall do no manner of servile work therein. . . And
> on the seventh day ye shall have an holy convoca-
> tion; ye shall do no servile work. (Nu. 28:17-25)*
>
> *. . . and on the seventh day shall be a solemn
> assembly to the LORD thy God: thou shalt do no work
> therein. (Deut. 16:18)*

Sacrifices: On each of the seven days of eating unleavened
bread, the 15th through the 21st Nisan, other animals were
sacrificed (besides the passover lambs offered on the 14th):

> *Thou shalt keep the feast of unleavened bread. . . and
> none shall appear before me empty. (Ex. 23:14)*
>
> *Ye shall offer an offering made by fire unto the LORD
> seven days. (Lev. 23:8)*
>
> *But ye shall offer a sacrifice made by fire for a
> burnt offering unto the LORD; two young bullocks,*

*and one ram, and seven lambs of the first year: they
shall be unto you without blemish: and their meat
offering shall be of flour mingled with oil; three
tenth deals shall ye offer for a bullock, and two tenth
deals for a ram; a several tenth deal shalt thou offer
for every lamb, throughout the seven lambs: and one
goat for a sin offering, to make an atonement for
you. Ye shall offer these beside the burnt offering in
the morning, which is for a continual burnt offering.
After this manner ye shall offer daily, throughout
the seven days, the meat of the sacrifice made by
fire, of a sweet savour unto the LORD: it shall be
offered beside the continual burnt offering, and his
drink offering. (Nu. 28:19-24)*

The special daily burnt offerings for the week of unleavened
bread were, in summary:

- 2 flawless young bullocks, each with a meal
  offering of 9 quarts of fine flour mixed with oil
- 1 flawless ram with a meal offering of 6 quarts
  fine flour mixed with oil
- 7 flawless yearling lambs, each with a meal
  offering of 3 quarts of fine flour mixed with oil
- 1 male goat for a sin offering to make
  atonement for all the people

These special offerings were to be offered in addition to the
daily burnt offerings:

- 1 flawless yearling lamb, with a meal offering of
  3 quarts fine flour mixed with oil. Plus a drink
  offering of 3 pints of strong wine poured out
  before the Lord. (The morning offering)
- 1 flawless yearling lamb, with a meal offering of
  3 quarts fine flour mixed with oil. Plus a drink
  offering of 3 pints of strong wine poured out

before the Lord. (The evening offering)
(Nu. 28:1-8)

For the Sabbath that would fall on one of the days of eating unleavened bread, an offering in addition to the regular morning and evening offerings and special offerings of the feast of unleavened bread was required:

- 2 flawless male yearling lambs, with a meal offering of a total of 6 quarts of fine flour mixed with oil. Plus a drink offering of a total of 6 pints of strong wine poured out before the Lord. (Nu. 28:9-10)

The ceremony of the passover sacrifice on the 14th Nisan and the ceremony of eating unleavened bread on the 15th through the 21st, while technically two separate institutions with distinct emphases, were together one great observance. Their meanings were interrelated and intertwined; they came together in the Passover meal on the 15th. They also came together in the other sacrifices to be offered during the week of eating unleavened bread. In times to come, the entire eight days would be called "The Passover" or "The Feast" or "The Feast of Unleavened Bread."

3

GREAT JOY IN JERUSALEM

And the children of Israel that were present in Jerusalem kept the feast of unleavened bread seven days with great gladness. . . And all the congregation of Judah, with the priests and Levites, and all the congregation that came out of Israel, and the strangers that came out of the land of Israel, and that dwelt in Judah, rejoiced. So there was great joy in Jerusalem.

(II Chron. 30:21,25-26)

It is not known how completely Israel obeyed God and kept the Passover through all the centuries of spiritual ups and downs recorded in the Old Testament. It seems there was always a faithful remnant and there were always those who disobeyed.

God had commanded annual observance of Passover, but even under Moses's leadership there were those who did not keep God's commands. Circumcision was commanded; it was a pre-requisite for keeping Passover (Ex. 12:43-49; Lev. 12:3). Yet no one born during the forty years of wilderness wanderings had been circumcised (Josh. 5:5-7). During long periods of apostasy, God's people neglected Passover (e.g., II Chron. 30:5). But when the people obeyed and observed it they experienced great gladness and rejoicing.

There are six Old Testament references to Passover observance:

- In the wilderness under Moses, about 1438 B.C. (Nu. 9:1-14)
- At Gilgal under Joshua, about 1400 B.C. (Josh. 5:10-12)
- At Jerusalem under Solomon, about 950-930 B.C. (II Chron. 8:13-15)

- At Jerusalem under Hezekiah, about 724 B.C. (II Chron. 30:1-27)
- At Jerusalem under Josiah, about 622 B.C. (II Ki. 23:21-23; II Chron. 35:1-19)
- At Jerusalem under Ezra, about 516 B.C. (Ezra 6:19-22)

Observance Under Moses and Joshua

Moses: In the first month of the second year after Israel came out of Egypt (about 1438 B.C.), the Lord spoke to Moses in the wilderness of Sinai and said to keep the Passover (Nu. 9:1-2). Moses and the people obeyed. This instance is recorded because of the special problem that arose at that time and the new regulations God gave to handle it.

Certain men were ritually defiled by contact with a dead body which made them ineligible to keep the Passover at the appointed time. This was the occasion on which the Lord gave the instructions for the second-month Passover. God said all those unable to keep Passover at the proper time were to keep it in the following month according to all the regulations and ordinances He had given for the regular Passover. The Lord emphasized, by repetition, four of those regulations: keep the Passover at evening, eat the passover lamb with unleavened bread and bitter herbs, leave none of it until morning, and break no bone of it (Nu. 9:6-12).

On this occasion God spoke the stern words that anyone who was able to keep the Passover but willfully chose not to was to be cut off from the people of God. He must "bear his sin" (Nu. 9:13) The Lord also said once again that if a stranger wanted to keep the Passover, he was to keep it with Israel according to all the ordinances God had given (Nu. 9:13).

Joshua: The next recorded instance of Passover observance takes place 38 years later. Moses had died and Joshua had taken his place as leader. The people had just entered the land on the 10th day of the first month (the day the passover lambs were to be selected and put aside until the 14th), about 1400 B.C. On that day Israel had miraculously entered the Promised Land from the east by crossing the Jordan River while God held back the waters as He had held back the waters of the Sea. Just ahead lay Jericho. The people camped at Gilgal in the plains of Jericho, just east of the city (Josh. 3 and 4).

There God ordered Joshua to have all the men of Israel circumcised. Those who had come out of Egypt (all now dead) had been circumcised, but all who had been born during the 40 years of wandering were uncircumcised. When they obeyed in this, the Lord said that on that day He rolled away the reproach of Egypt from the people. On the 14th, they observed the Passover (Josh. 5:2-10).

The unleavened bread Israel ate that Passover in Gilgal was made from the grain of the Promised Land. That very day as Israel ate the bread of the Promised Land, the manna which had sustained them in their wanderings ceased and never appeared again (Josh. 5:11-12).

Passover in Jerusalem

Scripture does not record any Passover observances during the period of Judges. Quite probably it was neglected during the many periods of apostasy. Already in Joshua's day the people were turning to other gods and forsaking God's Law (Josh. 24:23). Reference is made in Scripture to Passover observance at Jerusalem under the kings, however.

Solomon: Simple reference is made to the fact that the people kept Passover when Solomon was king, during the years between about 950-930 B.C. after his Temple had been completed (II Chron. 8:13-15). No details are given to describe observance in his day. Solomon was the third and last king of the United Kingdom. When he died, the ten northern tribes formed the Kingdom of Israel, and the two southern tribes formed the Kingdom of Judah. Rehoboam, King of Judah, and Jeroboam,

King of Israel, both led their people into wicked heathenism.

Hezekiah: About 200 years later, Hezekiah became king over the Southern Kingdom, Judah. In the first year of his reign, in the first month (the month in which Passover was to be observed), Hezekiah reopened the doors to the Temple and repaired them, for Israel had forsaken the Lord and His house some time earlier (II Chron. 29:1-7). Hezekiah gathered the priests and Levites and reestablished the sacrifices and Temple service (II Chron. 29).

Then Hezekiah sent letters via messengers throughout all Judah, Israel, Ephraim, and Manasseh telling the people to come to Jerusalem to observe the Passover (in the second month because there was not time for the priests to become sanctified and the people to arrive in Jerusalem for the regular first-month observance). Passover had not been observed in the proper way or by all the people for ''a long time'' (II Chron. 30:5)—not since Solomon (II Chron. 30:26).

It was a perilous time. Assyria had been waging military campaigns against the two nations (and did defeat the Northern Kingdom of Israel and take them away captive in 722 B.C.). Hezekiah urged all the people to turn back to the Lord and come observe Passover. His messengers were mocked and scorned as they went from city to city. Nevertheless many people from Asher, Manasseh and Zebulun ''humbled themselves and came to Jerusalem.'' God gave Judah ''one heart'' to obey Him. So a great number of people assembled in Jerusalem to observe a second-month passover. First they destroyed all the altars to pagan gods (II Chron. 30:1-14).

Then they killed the passovers on the 14th of the second month. The observance was irregular. It had been delayed until the second month because not all the priests and Levites had been sanctified. Even by the second month, not all in the congregation were sanctified for Temple worship according to the Law. Therefore the Levites, instead of the heads of the households, killed the passover lambs. As had become the rule for all animal sacrifices, the priests handled the blood of the sacrifice. With Passover at the Temple, the passovers' blood was sprinkled at the altar instead of applied to the doors of the houses. The people were not supposed to eat the passover if they were ritually unclean, but a multitude did. Hezekiah prayed and asked God to pardon them because they had prepared their hearts to seek Him. The Lord answered Hezekiah's prayer and "healed the people" (II Chron. 30:15-20).

The celebration of the Feast for the seven days of unleavened bread was marked by great gladness. The Levites and priests praised the Lord daily, singing with loud instruments. The people offered peace offerings and gave thanks and praise to the Lord.

It was such a joyful time that the whole assembly voted to extend the feast another seven days. Hezekiah gave thousands of animals to the people to continue the feast. All the people who kept that Passover rejoiced together — those from Judah and Israel, and those "strangers" not born of Israel's blood line. There was "great joy in Jerusalem." When the priests (who had not been leading the people aright until Hezekiah's revival) rose to bless the people, their prayers were heard of God (II Chron. 30:21-27).

Josiah: The next recorded Passover observance is the great Passover of the spiritual revival led by Josiah, 100 years later. The people had again become apostate. Josiah became king of Judah in 639 B.C. as an 8-year-old. When he was 16 he began to seek the Lord; when 20, he began purging Judah of the pagan religious practices that had once again taken hold in the land. At age 26 Josiah commissioned repairs to the Temple. Those in charge of the repairs found the scroll of the Law and read it to King Josiah. He tore his clothes in the Hebrew gesture of remorse when he heard the Law that the people were not keeping. He read the Word of God to the leaders, renewed covenant with God, and led the people into obedience. In 620 B.C. he renewed Passover observance after returning the Ark of the Covenant to the Temple (II Chron. 34-35).

For the Passover, Josiah instructed the clans of the Levites to resume their particular stations and duties of Temple service as designated by King David. (See I Chron. 23-26.) Josiah instructed the priests and Levites to sanctify themselves according to the Law, so they could kill the passovers. Josiah personally donated 30,000 lambs and kids and 3,000 cattle, and his officials donated 7,600 lambs and 800 cattle for this Passover observance (II Chron. 35:1-9).

As in Hezekiah's day, the Levites killed and flayed the passover animals, and the priests sprinkled the blood. The people offered other donated animals as burnt offerings. They roasted the passover lambs according to the Law, and boiled the other offerings (II Chron. 35:10-13).

The Levitical singers, the sons of Asaph, were at their stations singing and praising God with instruments as designated by David (I Chron. 23:30-31); doorkeepers were stationed in their places; other Levites prepared the ceremonial food for the priests, singers and doorkeepers (II Chron. 35:14-15).

The men of Israel who came to Jerusalem to observe the Passover at this time took part in what Scripture says was the greatest Passover since the days of the Judges—since the days of Samuel the prophet. None of the kings of Israel had kept such a Passover (II Chron. 35:18-19; II Kings 23:21-23).

A prophetess had told Josiah that God's judgment, about to fall upon Judah, would be delayed for his lifetime because he followed after the Lord (II Chron. 34:20-28). As long as Josiah was alive, he led the people to follow the Lord (II Chron. 34:33). When he died in battle at the untimely age of 39, the chief priests and people turned away from God and adopted the abominations of the heathen. They again polluted the Temple and mocked the prophets who warned them of judgment and tried to turn them back to the Lord. God's judgment fell in 586 B.C. The Babylonians destroyed Jerusalem, including the Temple, and took the people captive to Babylon.

Ezra: During the 70 years of Babylonian captivity there was no Passover. Because of the decree of Cyrus the Persian who defeated Babylon and released the captives, the children of Israel returned to Jerusalem to rebuild the walls of the city and the Temple, led by Nehemiah and Ezra.

Between 520-516 B.C. they completed the Temple and resumed Passover. Those who ovserved the 516 B.C. Passover included children of Israel returning from captivity and also "those from other nations who had separated themselves unto Israel from the filthiness of the heathen of the land to follow the Lord God of Israel." They "kept the feast with joy for the Lord had made they joyful" (Ezra 6:19-22).

4

EVERY YEAR AT THE FEAST

*Now his parents went to Jerusalem every year at the feast
of the passover. And when he was twelve years old, they
went up to Jerusalem after the custom of the feast.*
(Luke 2:41-42)

Israel regularly observed Passover in Jesus' day. Among those
faithful at the Feast every year were Mary and Joseph, the
parents of Jesus (Lk. 2:41). Luke records an occasion when
Jesus as a 12-year-old went to the Feast with His parents. It
was after this Passover that He stayed behind to interact with
scholarly teachers in the Temple, unbeknown to Mary and
Joseph (Lk. 2:41-51). As an adult, Jesus also went to Jerusalem
for the Feast of the Passover (Jn. 2:12-23; Matt.. 26:17-21; Mk.
14:12-18; Lk 22:7-15; Jn. 12:12). Jesus' Last Supper with His
disciples was a Passover meal.

Details of what Passover was like in Jesus' day can be gleaned
from the Primary Documents—those historic writings,
especially the Bible, which were set down before 70 A.D. The
regulations of the Law (see Chapters 1 and 2) would still have
been binding at the time of the Last Supper. The Bible's
Historical Books speak of customs in addition to the Law which
might have been passed down to Jesus' day (see Chapter 3).
The Gospels contain more information. The Bible's details are
supplemented by data in the non-Biblical Primary Documents
(see Appendix 1). One can construct a composite of Passover
observance in Jesus' day by combining information from the
various primary sources.

A Joyful, Busy Pilgrim Feast

Passover was one of the three ''Pilgrim Feasts''—Passover,

Pentecost, and Tabernacles, for which all men of Israel were obliged to come to Jerusalem (Deut. 16:16; Ex. 23:14-17). In Jesus' day women and children—at least young boys, also came for Passover (Lk. 2:41-42).

Not only Jews, but also Gentiles who worshiped the God of Israel, observed Passover. The Apostle John writes of certain "Greeks" who came to Jerusalem to worship at the Feast of Passover (Jn. 12:20).

The ceremony of the Passover sacrifice and the week of eating unleavened bread were considered parts of one great feast. The entire eight days were variously called Passover or The Feast or The Feast of Unleavened Bread. The New Testament writers used these names interchangeably (Matt. 26:17; Mk. 14:1,12; Lk. 22:1,7). The first-century historian Josephus called the day of the Passover sacrifice "*Pascha*" (Passover), and the week of eating unleavened bread, The Feast of Unleavened Bread. In one place he makes a technical distinction between the *Pascha* and the week-long feast, yet uses the common custom, saying, ". . .the Feast of Unleavened Bread. . .which is called the *Pascha*."[1]

Jerusalem, the location of the Temple where God had "put His name," was the required place for observing Passover (Deut. 12 & 16). The small city was exceedingly crowded at Feast time; its boundaries in Jesus' day were not greater than 5/8 mile wide by 1 mile long. Josephus estimated that the number of pilgrims in Jerusalem for the 70 A.D. Passover was about 3 million: ". . .the number of sacrifices was two hundred and fifty-six thousand five hundred; which, upon the allowance of no more than ten that feast together, amounts to two millions seven hundred thousand and two hundred that were pure..."[2] Today's historians consider Josephus's estimate exaggerated (three million people within the city's boundaries would allow only 5.8 square feet per person—and that is if there were no buildings at all there!). But whatever the actual count of pilgrims, extreme crowdedness was certainly part of the scene. When Jesus went to Jerusalem for Passover, He entered the city daily, but left each night for lodging outside the city limits (Matt. 21:17-18; Mk. 11:11-12,19; Lk 21:37).

Pilgrims arrived in Jerusalem a week before the Passover. Josephus says they arrived on 8th Nisan. Jesus and His disciples entered Jerusalem for His last Passover 5 days before the Feast (Jn. 12:12). The people arrived early to allow more time for reunions and "vacation," but primarily to purify themselves ritually (Jn. 11:55).

The priests, Levites, and all the people had to be ritually pure according to the Law before they could participate in the Feast. Certain conditions required ritual acts and offerings for purification. These included the birth of a child (Lev. 12), contact with a deceased relative or other dead body (Nu. 19), certain diseases such as leprosy (Lev. 13) and uncleanness from a running sore (Lev. 15). Josephus mentions ritual impurity due to gonorrhea and menstruation. Purification rites involved the sacrifice of cattle, lambs, and turtledoves or pigeons.

Twice when sellers and money changers set up shop in the Temple itself to sell animals for purification rites Jesus drove them out (Jn. 2:13-23; Matt. 21:12; Mk. 11:15-17; Lk. 19:45-56) He quoted Isaiah 56:7 that the Temple was to be "a house of prayer for all peoples"—not a merchandise market, much less a den of thieves.

Josephus and *Megillath Ta'anith* (Appendix 1) speak of the pre-Feast purification rites. Those unable to fulfill purification in time for Passover, or those soldiers and others in a distant country unable to come to the Feast at the appointed time were to observe the second-month Passover (Nu. 9; II Chron. 30). People who ate the Passover without being sanctified were subject to the Lord's judgment—illness or death (II Chron. 30:20).

There was much activity to keep people busy the week before Passover and the week of the Feast. In addition to the purification ceremonies, there was presentation of tithes and offerings which the people brought to the Lord. There was daily service in the Temple. In addition to Temple worship, there were opportunities for people to cluster together in different places for teaching and discussion. Jesus taught in the Temple during the Feast (Matt. 21:23; Mk. 12:35; Lk. 19:47, 20:1). Feast time provided opportunity for reunion with family and friends.

The atmosphere of the week was informal and joyful. The book of *Jubilees* echos the accounts in Hezekiah's and Ezra's times that Passover was a joyful family feast (Appendix 1). *Megillath Ta'anith* speaks of the joyful atmosphere. It in fact considers joyfulness at Passover an obligation just as it was an obligation for the Feasts of Tabernacles and Pentecost (Lev. 23:40; Deut. 16:11-15). No fasting or mourning was allowed during the Feast. A spirit of generosity also seemed to prevail. The Last Supper reference to money gifts for the poor (Jn. 13:29) and the Roman custom of releasing a prisoner during Passover (Matt. 27:15; Mk. 15:6; Lk. 23:18; Jn. 18:39) represent charitable Passover custom.

The Passover Sacrifice

At the original Passover in Egypt, the passover lambs had to be selected on the 10th Nisan and set apart until their sacrifice on the 14th. When they had been sacrificed in Egypt, their blood was put on the doors of the houses. The Israelites in Egypt had to eat the passover lamb dressed in travel clothes ready to depart Egypt at a moment's notice. There is no further discussion in the Bible about the continuance of these three requirements. The author of *Questions and Answers to Genesis and Exodus* (Philo?) indicates that none of these practices were part of the observance by Jesus' time (see Appendix 1). For many centuries the blood of the passover lambs had been applied to the Temple altar at the door of the spiritual "house" of Israel.

The passover lambs, according to the Law, had to be flawless male yearlings from the sheep or goats. They had to be slain at that place where "God put His name," the place of meeting with Him—in Jesus' day, as it had been for centuries, the Temple in Jerusalem.

The passovers were sacrified "at even as the sun was setting." At the time of *Jubilees*, 135-105 B.C., the lambs were slain between 2-6 p.m. at the Temple. Josephus, c 37-100 A.D., records that they were then slain at the Temple between 3-5 p.m.

In Moses's day laymen sacrificed their own lambs. In Hezekiah's day Levites killed them because the laymen were unsanctified. In Josiah's day the Levites killed them. Philo, 20 B.C.-40 A.D., says laymen sacrificed the passovers (Appendix 1). The priests handled the blood, catching it in a basin and applying it to the altar. It is possible according to references in *Questions and Answers to Genesis and Exodus* that the required age of the lambs might have been necessarily altered by Jesus' day.

The sacrifice of the passovers at the Temple was the community observance required by the Law. It was a worship service ritual. As decreed by David, and illustrated in Josiah's Passover, doorkeepers and Levites with other duties were organized at various stations to perform their specific Temple services during the time the passovers were sacrificed. If the Levites did not kill and skin the animals, they did assist in that. Some of the Levites kept busy preparing food for the priests, doorkeepers, and singers. The Levitical singers (Sons of Asaph) stood at designated places singing and praising God with instruments while the passovers were sacrificed. The lambs were sacrificed in three shifts in Jesus' day. A *Mishnah* reference to Temple practice (pre 70 A.D.) says the Temple Levites sang the *Hallel* (Psalms 113-118) while the passovers were sacrificed. They repeated the *Hallel* if necessary.[3]

The Passover Meal

Because of the great multitude of people involved, some of the original laws about Passover **had** to be altered. ''The place where the Lord put His name'' had to be extended from the Temple boundaries to include the entire city of Jerusalem, inside the walls. Still in the days of *Jubilees*, 135-105 B.C., the Passover ritual meal was eaten in the Temple courts before 2:00 a.m. But by Jesus' day there simply was not room at the Temple, in the time allowed, for all the people to roast and eat the lambs there in addition to sacrificing them there.

Place Eaten: The Passover meal in Jesus' day was eaten in houses—at least by part of the people (Matt. 26:17-18; Mk. 14:12-14; Lk. 22:9-12, 29:11). Josephus writes that just after midnight the priests reopened the Temple gates. They were perhaps closed after the Passover sacrifices for clean up, then reopened so the needed Temple space could be used for eating by as many of the multitude as possible. The Temple with its courts occupied 15-20 percent of Jerusalem's total land area at that time. Considering the crowdedness and scarcity of places to eat, it is conceivable that many of Jerusalem's houses and other buildings could have been utilized by multiple groups. Possibly in some places the ritual meal was eaten in shifts.

Time Eaten: The passover ritual meal was eaten well into the night after the lamb had roasted whole for several hours. That dated the eating on ''the next day,'' the 15th Nisan by Jewish reckoning of days. The writer of *Questions and Answers to Genesis and Exodus* indicates a relaxation of the rule that the lamb be eaten only at night. Perhaps adjustment was necessary to allow for all in the great multitude of pilgrims to participate.

Custom, in the time of *Jubilees* had been that the meal be eaten in the Temple courts before 2 a.m., but by Jesus' time, about 150 years later, that customary deadline had been extended. God's command through Moses was that the passover lamb be consumed before **dawn** (Ex. 12:10).

Fratria: According to the writer of *Questions and Answers to Genesis and Exodus,* the Mosaic rule about a family combining with enough others to consume a lamb was interpreted in such a way as to meet the demanding circumstances of that day. Josephus describes the custom of eating the passover in group units called *fratria,* normally 10-20 people. Jesus, at table with the Twelve Apostles, comprised one such *fratria* (Matt. 26:20; Mk. 14:17; Lk. 22:14). The rest of Jesus' approximately 120 disciples, including relatives of His and the Apostles, could have formed other *fratria* in the same luxuriously-"**large**" upper room Jesus utilized when space was at such a premium (Mk. 14:15; Lk. 22:12). The Biblical text allows for, and possibly **calls for,** the inclusion of all Jesus' disciples at the Last Supper—all those who later gathered together at Pentecost (quite possibly in the same room used for the Last Supper). When Jesus told His disciples that one of them who was eating with Him would betray Him, they all asked "Is it I?" And He answered them saying, "It is **one of the twelve**" (Mk. 14:20). He did not answer, "Yes, I **said** it is one of **you**" as though He were speaking to only the twelve Apostles. It seems He said it was one of the Twelve (who dipped in His table's dish) as a way of narrowing the designation from the possibilities in the larger group. Then he further specified the very individual—the one to whom He gave the sop (Jn. 13:26).

Food Eaten: The food eaten at the Passover meal in Jesus' day was certainly the three foods required in the Law: the passover lamb, unleavened bread, and bitter herbs. Certainly the people kept the letter of the Law not to break a bone of the lamb or carry any of the meat from their house (or *fratria*) to another place.

Wine, while not instituted in the Law as part of the Passover meal, had become customary, and was used at the Last Supper (Matt. 26:27-29; Mark 14:23-25; Luke 22:18-20). It is first mentioned in *Jubilees* as being part of the celebration. Philo mentions it. It is prominent in the New Testament for the meaning Jesus gave to it at the Last Supper. Wine was a symbol of luxury; it was unaffordable for everyday use by common people. It was also a symbol of joy.

Passover Meal Ceremony: Not much is known about the ritual eating of the Passover meal in Jesus' day. Scholars are in general agreement, on the basis of information in the Primary Documents, that Passover in Jesus' day was far less regulated than the ritual laid down in the much-later *Haggadah*.[4] The ceremony of eating was far less formal than Passover seders of later centuries and today.

Passover participants in Jesus' time "reclined" after the ancient manner of eating in ease and luxury (Matt. 26:20; Lk. 22:14; Jn. 13:25).

There were places of honor at meals in Jesus' day; there were "chief places at feasts" (Matt. 23:6; Mk. 12:39; Lk. 11:43), perhaps at the Passover meal itself.

Jesus "broke bread" and gave it to His disciples at the Last Supper Passover (Matt. 26:26; Mk. 14:22; Lk. 22:19). That breaking of bread may have been a functional action with no significance other than what it would have had at any Hebrew meal, along with the meaning Jesus newly gave it. Or that breaking of bread may have been part of a first-century Passover ritual that Jesus endowed with new meaning. It simply is not known. There is no basis for saying conclusively that the bread breaking of later *Haggadah* ritual is a ceremony in which Jesus participated. It might have been; it might not have been.

A similar conclusion must be drawn about the cup of wine Jesus took and endowed with symbolic significance pertaining to His sacrificial death and the New Covenant. There may have been four ceremonial cups of wine drunk at Passover in Jesus' time as there was in the third-century *Mishnah*. On the other hand, there might not have been four cups in Jesus' day. The Bible does not say how many cups of wine were used ritually. In fact, the Bible does not indicate whether the wine was used ritually at all or whether it was simply part of the festive meal as it was part of other festive meals. The *Mishnah* does not indicate when the four-cup custom of which it speaks began. It certainly did not originate in the Law.

The "dipping in the dish" (Matt. 26:13 and Mark 14:20) might have been a ritual act or it might have been the simple functional activity of people at one table eating a common meal from the same dish(es). The dipping was mentioned in the Gospels to specify that one who ate with Jesus, in His own *fratria*, would betray Him. The sign of giving the sop to Judas after dipping (Jn. 13:26) further designated the specific individual who would betray Jesus. That sop could well have been a portion of lamb with unleavened bread and bitter herbs— possibly dipped ritually; possibly not dipped ritually. Or the sop could have been some other food.

The *Mishnah* says the *Hallel* (Psalms 113-118) was sung at the Temple as the passovers were sacrificed. Those Psalms were possibly, but not necessarily, also sung at the people's homes during the passover meal. The Bible says Jesus and His disciples sang "**a** hymn." It does not use wording such as "**the** hymn" which would link the song to an established ritual.

Passover in Jesus' day was apparently an all-night feast. The word in Deuteronomy about the people returning to their tents in the morning (Deut. 16:7), the New Testament descriptions of people being up at all hours of the night on Passover (e.g., Jn. 18), and the probability of the multitude of pilgrims requiring extra time for all to eat, seem to bear this out.

The Week-Long Feast: The Passover ceremony on the 14th Nisan was followed by eating the passover on the 15th (at night—which was actually early in the day by Jewish time reckoning). The Passover meal early on the 15th began the seven days of eating unleavened bread and offering additional sacrifices (see Chapter 2.)

On the first and seventh days of Unleavened Bread (viz. the 15th and 21st Nisan) there were religious assemblies of the gathered nation of Israel. No menial work could be done on those convocation days. According to the Law, the only work that could be done was that which was required for the feast.

While the week-long peace offerings of the people and the required daily sacrifices for the Feast of Unleavened Bread were being offered in the Temple, the Levites and priests daily praised God with singing and instruments. The priests pronounced blessings upon the people.

In addition to the people's individual offerings, the daily burnt offerings on behalf of the nation during the Feast included 2 bulls, 1 ram, 7 lambs, and 1 goat for a sin offering. These were offered with meal offerings (actually unleavened bread offerings of flour and oil.) In addititon to these offerings there were the regular morning and evening sacrifices — a lamb with a meal offering and a poured-out wine drink offering sacrificed every morning and every evening of the year. Further, there was the additional Sabbath offering of 2 lambs with a meal offering and a poured-out wine offering for the Sabbath which fell during the Feast. More animal sacrifices were required during this Feast than at any other time in the year.

The Day of Firstfruits: The Lord had also instituted a special observance for "the morrow after the Sabbath" (the Sunday) that fell during the Feast. On that day the nation of Israel was to bring a sheaf of the firstfruits of the barley harvest to the priest who would "wave" it before the Lord. At that time of waving the Firstfruits sheaf, there was to be a sacrifice of a flawless male yearling lamb, offered as a burnt offering along with a meal offering of about one fifth bushel of fine flour mixed with oil and a drink offering of about three pints of wine.

On that day of harvest "Firstfruits," Israel was to "count from the morrow after the sabbath, from the day that ye brought the sheaf of the wave offering; seven sabbaths shall be complete: even unto the morrow after the seventh sabbath shall ye number fifty days" (Lev. 23:9-16). The 50th day after the Sunday of Firstfruits was the Feast of Shavuot, also called the Feast of Weeks and Pentecost, a feast of the full harvest. By having the people count the weeks from Passover to Pentecost, the Lord linked the two feasts.

Footnotes:

[1]Flavius Josephus, *Antiquities of the Jews*, xvii, ix, 3.

[2]Josephus, *Wars of the Jews*, vi, ix, 3.

[3]*Mishnah*, Pesachim 5:5-7. (The *Mishnah* is the authoritative voice of Rabbinical Judaism codified about 200-250 A.D.)

[4]The *Haggadah* is the Jewish Passover ritual used today. Rooted in the *Mishnah* of the 3rd century, it has evolved over many centuries, finally being fixed in its present form in the 10th century.

5

REMEMBER NOT THE FORMER THINGS

*Thus saith the LORD. which maketh a way in the sea,
and a path in the mighty waters; which bringeth forth
the chariot and the horse, the army and the power
. . . Remember ye not the former things, neither consider
the things of old. Behold, I will do a new thing.*

(Is. 43:16-19)

The Lord commanded Israel to remember forever that He had redeemed them from Egypt and delivered them from bondage. He Himself constantly kept that fact before them. Over and over He repeated through His prophets, "I am the Lord thy God which brought thee out of the land of Egypt, from the house of bondage." Most of the Old Testament books contain direct reference or allusion to that mighty deliverance.

And yet, as great and worthy of remembrance as that redemption was, the Lord said He would do a new thing that would make that magnificent deliverance from Egypt pale in comparison:

> *Thus saith the LORD, which maketh a way in the
> sea, and a path in the mighty waters; which
> bringeth forth the chariot and horse, the army and
> the power. . . Remember ye not the former things,
> neither consider the things of old. Behold, I will do a
> new thing.*   *(Is. 43:16-19)*

What would this new thing be? Another Exodus? This time from Assyria? Miraculous plagues upon Babylon? Deliverance from yet-future oppressors? Whatever else God would do intervening in worldly events, He primarily had in mind something far more wonderful:

53

I will ransom them from the power of the grave;
I will redeem them from death: O death, I will be
thy plagues; O grave, I will be thy destruction.

(Hos. 13:14)

Redemption From Death

At a specific place on earth—the mountain of Jerusalem—
God would defeat death. In that, He would make a feast for
all mankind celebrating eternal life—an infinitely-greater salvation than Israel's salvation from Egypt:

And in this mountain shall the LORD of hosts make
unto all people a feast. . . And he will destroy in this
mountain the face of the covering cast over all
people, and the vail that is spread over all nations.
He will swallow up death in victory; and the LORD
will wipe away tears from off all faces. (Is. 25: 6-8)

In ancient times, God gave glimpses of this redemption to
men of faith:

For I know that my redeemer liveth, and that he
shall stand at the latter day upon the earth: and
though after my skin worms destroy this body, yet in
my flesh shall I see God: whom I shall see for
myself, and mine eyes shall behold, and not another;
though my reins be consumed within me.

(Job 19:25-27)

God will redeem my soul from the power of the
grave: for he shall receive me. (Psalms 49:15)

Thy dead men shall live, together with my dead
body shall they arise. Awake and sing, ye that dwell
in dust. (Is. 26:19)

And many of them that sleep in the dust of the earth
shall awake, some to everlasting life, and some to
shame and everlasting contempt. (Dan. 12:2)

With the same compassion that He looked upon Israel under Egyptian slavery, The Creator has looked upon all mankind held in bondage to death. He who has all power, mercy, and grace has heard man's cries for deliverance:

> *This shall be written for the generation to come: and the people which shall be created shall praise the LORD. For he hath looked down from the height of his sanctuary; from heaven did the LORD behold the earth; to hear the groaning of the prisoner; to loose those that are appointed to death.*   *(Ps. 102:18-20)*

No man has the means to redeem, to buy back, from death any other man. All the treasures of earth combined could not bring back one soul from death:

> *None of them can by any means redeem his brother, nor give to God a ransom for him: (For the redemption of their soul is precious, and it ceaseth for ever:) that he should still live for ever, and not see corruption.*   *(Ps. 49:7-9)*

But God (the Redeemer) could pay Himself (the Judge) the ransom price to redeem man from death—and He would:

> *God will redeem my soul from the power of the grave: for he shall receive me.*   *(Ps. 49:15)*

Redemption From Sin

Death passed upon men in Eden because Adam and Eve transgressed God's command not to eat of the tree of knowledge of good and evil (Gen. 2:15-3:24). God said that if they ate of that tree they would surely die (Gen. 2:17). When they disobeyed, God took the tree of life away from man (Gen. 3:22-24).

Since Eden, all men have transgressed God's commands— all have disobediently stepped over lines He has drawn by His Law. Men have done that which God said they ought not to have done. Since Eden, all men have sinned: all have fallen short of the letter of God's Law—not to mention the spirit of the Law. Men have failed to do that which God said they ought to do.

God's standards are high. The Law He gave Israel when He brought them out of Egypt to be His holy people demands complete and perfect allegience to Him:

> *Thou shalt love the LORD thy God with all thine*
> *heart, and with all thy soul, and with all thy might.*
> *(Deut. 6:5). . . diligently keep all these*
> *commandments which I command you, to do them,*
> *to love the LORD your God, to walk in all His ways,*
> *and to cleave unto him. . .*   *(Deut. 11:22)*

His judgment for failure to keep the spirit and letter of His law is severe:

> *Behold, I set before you this day a blessing and a*
> *curse; a blessing if ye obey the commandments of the*
> *LORD your God, which I command you this day: and*
> *a curse, if ye will not obey the commandments of the*
> *LORD your God, but turn aside out of the way which*
> *I command you this day.*   *(Deut. 11:26-28)*
> *Cursed be he that confirmeth not [all] the words of*
> *this law to do them. And all the people shall say,*
> *Amen.*   *(Deut. 27:26)*

There is life in righteousness (Lev. 18:5, Deut. 6:2; Ezek. 18:5-22. See also Lk. 10:25-28); there would be eternal life in perfect righteousness. But all have fallen far short of God's standard, and therefore all die:

> *When I say to the righteous, that he shall surely live;*
> *if he trust to his own righteousness, and commit*
> *iniquity, all his righteousnesses shall not be*
> *remembered; but for his iniquity that he hath*
> *committed, he shall die for it.*   *(Ezek. 33:13)*

*We are all as an unclean thing, and all our
righteousnesses are as a filthy rag; and we do fade
as a leaf; and our iniquities, like the wind, have
taken us away.* (Is. 64:6)

*Enter not into judgment with thy servant: for in thy
sight shall no man living be justified.* (Ps. 143:2)

*The heart is deceitful above all things, and
desperately wicked.* (Jer. 17:9)

*There is not a just man upon earth, that doeth good,
and sinneth not (Eccl. 7:20). There is no man that
sinneth not (I Ki. 8:46; II Chron. 6:36). God looked
down from heaven upon the children of men, to see
if there were any that did understand, that did seek
God. Every one of them is gone back: they are
altogether become filthy; there is none that doeth
good, no, not one. (Ps. 53:2,3).*

The soul that sinneth, it shall die. (Ezek. 18:4,20)
Everyone shall die for his own iniquity. (Jer. 31:30)

Defeating death involves defeating sin. The tree of life was
taken away from Adam and Eve after they disobeyed God, lest
they live forever in their state of sin. The prophets proclaimed
the good news that God would defeat sin just as surely as He
had redeemed His people from the death plague in Egypt and
just as surely as He had defeated the Egyptian army at the
Red Sea:

*Who is a God like unto thee, that pardoneth
iniquity, and passeth by the transgression of the
remnant of his heritage? He retaineth not his anger
for ever, because he delighteth in mercy. He will turn
again, he will have compassion upon us; he will
subdue our iniquities; and thou wilt cast all their
sins into the depths of the sea.* (Micah 7:18-19)

*I am the LORD, your Holy One, the creator of Israel,
your King. Thus saith the LORD, which maketh a*

> *way in the sea, and a path in the mighty waters;*
> *which bringeth forth the chariot and horse, the army*
> *and the power. . . Behold, I will do a new thing; now*
> *it shall spring forth; shall ye not know it? I will even*
> *make a way in the wilderness, and rivers in the*
> *desert. . . This people have I formed for myself; they*
> *shall shew forth my praise. . . I, even I, am he that*
> *blotteth out thy transgressions for mine own sake,*
> *and will not remember thy sins.*　　　*(Is. 43:15-25)*

The Sin Bearer

In Egypt, the firstborn were redeemed by the blood of the passover lambs. The passover lambs bore God's death judgment in the tenth plague instead of Israel's firstborn. The passover sacrifice was the forerunner of other sacrifices instituted in the Law.

The sacrifices of the Law were God's provision for Israel to make peace with Him and reestablish fellowship broken by sin. (God is "of purer eyes than to behold evil, and canst not look on iniquity," Hab. 1:13. "Your iniquities have separated between you and your God, and your sins have hid his face from you, that he will not hear." Is. 59:2) Atonement for sin required blood sacrifice. (See also Leviticus 16 on the Day of Atonement.)

When the people laid their hands upon the sacrifice animals, they symbolized the transfer of sin. The animals representing the bearing of their sin died in their place, bearing the judgment for sin:

> *Wherefore have ye not eaten the sin offering in the*
> *holy place, seeing it is most holy, and God hath*
> *given it you to bear the iniquity of the congregation,*
> *to make atonement for them before the LORD?*
> 　　　　　　　　　　　　　　　　　*(Lev. 10: 17)*

> *For the life of the flesh is in the blood: and I have*
> *given it to you upon the altar to make an atonement*

for your souls: for it is the blood that maketh an
atonement for the soul. (Lev. 17:11)

The blood of the sin bearers was put upon the altar, at the door of the Tabernacle (Lev. 4:18), just as the passover lamb's blood was put upon the doors of the houses in Egypt:

And he shall put some of the blood upon the horns
of the altar which is before the LORD, that is in the
tabernacle of the congregation, and shall pour out all
the blood at the bottom of the altar of the burnt
offering, which is at the door of the tabernacle of the
congregation... And the priest shall take of the
blood of the sin offering with his finger, and put it
upon the horns of the altar of burnt offering, and
shall pour out all the blood thereof at the bottom of
the altar... and the priest shall make an atonement
for his sin that he hath committed, and it shall be
forgiven him. (Lev. 4:18, 34-35)

It was not because he wanted the slaughter of animals that God instituted blood sacrifice; it was because He wanted righteousness:

For I desired mercy, and not sacrifice; and the
knowledge of God more than burnt offerings.
(Hosea 6:6)

To do justice and judgment is more acceptable to the
LORD than sacrifice. (Prov. 21:3)

For thou desirest not sacrifice; else would I give it:
thou delightest not in burnt offering. The sacrifices of
God are a broken spirit: a broken and a contrite
heart, O God, thou wilt not despise. (Ps. 51:16-17)

Yet He did command the sacrifices. The people did not attain to His requirements of mercy, justice, knowledge of God, and contriteness over sin, so the sacrifices had to be offered endlessly—morning and evening, on the Sabbath, on the Day of Atonement and the other feasts—sin offerings, trespass offerings, peace offerings, purification offerings, over and over and over again. If the sacrifice of animals did not impart righteousness, and it was not what God wanted, why did He institute it? A Messianic prophecy in one of David's psalms provides an insight. The sacrifices were related to a coming one who *was* righteous, who had God's law within his heart:

> *Sacrifice and offering thou didst not desire; mine ears hast thou opened: burnt offering and sin offering has thou not required.*
>
> *Then said I, Lo, I come: in the volume of the book it is written of me, I delight to do thy will, O my God: yea, thy law is within my heart.* (Ps. 40:6-8)

The prophet Isaiah who saw so much of the Lord's "new thing" foresaw this righteous individual as one who would bear the transgressions and iniquity of all men. This "lamb brought to the slaughter" would die for people with their sins upon him. But he would live again. Because he would bear the iniquities of sinners, he would justify them before the Lord. This one who would be the ultimate sin bearer was the Lord's highly-exalted servant, the Messiah:

> *Behold, my servant shall deal prudently, he shall be exalted and extolled, and be very high.*
>
> *As many were astonished at thee; his visage was so marred more than any man, and his form more than the sons of men: So shall he sprinkle many nations; the kings shall shut their mouths at him: for that which had not been told them shall they see; and that which they had not heard shall they consider. Who hath believed our report? and to whom is the arm of the LORD revealed?*

*For he shall grow up before him as a tender plant,
and as a root out of a dry ground: he hath no form
nor comeliness; and when we shall see him, there is
no beauty that we should desire him. He is despised
and rejected of men; a man of sorrows, and
acquainted with grief: and we hid as it were our
faces from him; he was despised, and we esteemed
him not.*

*Surely he hath borne our griefs, and carried our
sorrows: yet we did esteem him stricken, smitten of
God, and afflicted. But he was wounded for our
transgressions, he was bruised for our iniquities: the
chastisement of our peace was upon him; and with
his stripes we are healed. All we like sheep have
gone astray; we have turned every one to his own
way; and the LORD hath laid on him the iniquity of
us all.*

*He was oppressed, and he was afflicted, yet he
opened not his mouth: he is brought as a lamb to the
slaughter, and as a sheep before her shearers is
dumb, so he openeth not his mouth. He was taken
from prison and from judgment: and who shall
declare his generation? for he was cut off out of the
land of the living: for the transgression of my people
was he stricken. and he made his grave with the
wicked, and with the rich in his death; because he
had done no violence, neither was any deceit in his
mouth. Yet it pleased the LORD to bruise him; he
hath put him to grief:*

*when thou shalt make his soul an offering for sin,
he shall see his seed, he shall prolong his days, and
the pleasure of the LORD shall prosper in his hand.
He shall see of the travail of his soul, and shall be
satisfied: by his knowledge shall my righteous
servant justify many; for he shall bear their
iniquities. Therefore will I divide him a portion with*

> *the great, and he shall divide the spoil with the*
> *strong; because he hath poured out his soul unto*
> *death: and he was numbered with the transgressors;*
> *and he bare the sin of many, and made intercession*
> *for the transgressors.* (Isaiah 52:13-53:12)

The New Covenant

Through His prophets, God spoke often of establishing His people in righteousness. At times He alluded to the deliverance from Egypt, using it as a similitude to tell about the utimate redemption He had prepared. He told of a new covenant He would make with Israel (who had broken the old covenant). He spoke of imparting His own righteousness to men and pouring out His Spirit upon them:

> *Behold, the days come, saith the LORD, that I will*
> *make a new covenant with the house of Israel, and*
> *with the house of Judah: not according to the*
> *covenant that I made with their fathers in the day*
> *that I took them by the hand to bring them out of*
> *the land of Egypt; which my covenant they brake,*
> *although I was an husband unto them, saith the*
> *LORD: But this shall be the covenant that I will make*
> *with the house of Israel; After those days, saith the*
> *LORD I will put my law in their inward parts, and*
> *write it in their hearts; and will be their God, and*
> *they shall be my people. And they shall teach no*
> *more every man his neighbour, and every man his*
> *brother, saying, Know the LORD: for they shall all*
> *know me, from the least of them unto the greatest of*
> *them, saith the LORD: For I will forgive their*
> *iniquity, and I will remember their sin no more.*
> (Jer. 31:31-34)

> *With everlasting kindness will I have mercy on thee,*
> *saith the Lord thy Redeemer...my kindness shall*
> *not depart from thee, neither shall the covenant of*
> *my peace be removed, saith the LORD that hath*

mercy on thee. . . In righteousness shalt thou be established. . . This is the heritage of the servants of the LORD, and their righteousness is of me, saith the LORD.   (Is. 54:8,10,14,17)

And the LORD thy God will circumcise thine heart, and the heart of thy seed, to love the LORD thy God with all thine heart, and with all thy soul, that thou mayest live.   (Deut. 30:6)

Thus saith the LORD, which maketh a way in the sea, and a path in the mighty waters. . . I will even make a way in the wilderness, and rivers in the desert, to give drink to my people, my chosen. . . For I will pour water upon him that is thirsty, and floods upon the dry ground: I will pour my spirit upon thy seed, and my blessing upon thine offspring. . . Ho, every one that thirsteth, come ye to the waters. . . Incline your ear, and come unto me: hear, and your soul shall live; and I will make an everlasting covenant with you, even the sure mercies of David.   (Is. 43:16,19,20; 44:3; 55:1,3)

And it shall come to pass afterward, that I will pour out my spirit upon all flesh; and your sons and your daughters shall prophesy, your old men shall dream dreams, your young men shall see visions; And also upon the servants and upon the handmaids in those days will I pour out my spirit. . . And it shall come to pass, that whosoever shall call on the name of the LORD shall be delivered: for in Mount Zion and in Jerusalem shall be deliverance, as the LORD hath said, and in the remnant whom the LORD shall call. (Joel 2:28-29, 32)

I will save them out of all their dwellingplaces, wherein they have sinned, and will cleanse them: so shall they be my people, and I will be their God. And David my servant shall be king over them; and

they all shall have one shepherd: they shall also
walk in my statutes, and do them. . . and my servant
David shall be their prince for ever. Moreover I will
make a covenant of peace with them; it shall be an
everlasting covenant with them. (Ezek. 37:23-26)

The Messiah and Righteousness

The days of the New Covenant salvation spoken of by the prophets are the days of Messiah. The Messianic passages bring out the Lord's emphasis on salvation having to do with righteousness. Yes, God would help His people when they were troubled and oppressed by others. But the greatest salvation He could give is delivering the world from evil and death. To do that, God deals with the evil in the heart of each and every person. Ezekiel's prophecies about cleansing from sin and the everlasting covenant of peace say that "David" (a word for Messiah, since David died before Ezekiel's time) would reign during the time of this salvation—this establishing people in God's own righteousness (Ezek. 37:21-28) Hosea and Isaiah also proclaim this (Hos. 3:5, Is. 55:1-3), as do Jeremiah and Daniel:

Behold, the days come, saith the LORD, that I will
raise unto David a righteous Branch, and a King
shall reign and prosper, and shall execute judgment
and justice in the earth. In his days Judah shall be
saved, and Israel shall dwell safely: and this is his
name whereby he shall be called, THE LORD OUR
RIGHTEOUSNESS. Therefore, behold, the days come,
saith the LORD, that they shall no more say The LORD
liveth, which brought up the children of Israel out of
the land of Egypt; But, the LORD liveth, which
brought up and which led the seed of the house of
Israel out of the north country, and from all
countries whither I had driven them; and they shall
dwell in their own land.   (Jer. 23:5-8)

Seventy weeks are determined upon thy people and

upon thy holy city, to finish the transgression, and
to make an end of sins, and to make reconciliation
for iniquity, and to bring in everlasting righteous-
ness, and to seal up the vision and prophecy, and to
anoint the most Holy. Know therefore and under-
stand that from the going forth of the commandment
to restore and to build Jerusalem unto the Messiah
the Prince shall be seven weeks, and threescore and
two weeks: the streets shall be built again, and the
wall, even in troublous times. And after threescore
and two weeks shall Messiah be cut off, but not for
himself: and the people of the prince that shall come
shall destroy the city and the sanctuary and the end
thereof shall be with a flood, and unto the end of the
war desolations are determined. And he shall
confirm the covenant with many for one week: and
in the midst of the week he shall cause the sacrifice
and the oblation to cease, and for the overspreading
of abominations he shall make it desolate, even until
the consumation, and that determined shall be
poured upon the desolate.   *(Dan. 9:24-27)*

And the Redeemer shall come to Zion, and unto
them that turn from transgression in Jacob, saith the
LORD. As for me, this is my covenant with them,
saith the LORD; My spirit is upon thee, and my
words which I have put in thy mouth, shall not
depart out of thy mouth, nor out of the mouth of thy
seed's seed, saith the LORD, from henceforth and for
ever.   *(Is. 59:20,21)*

The Glory of Israel, the Messiah, would bring honor to the
Lord throughout the earth. Messiah, God's Perfect Servant and
the Sinbearer, would extend the covenant of God's salvation
to all men:

Neither let the son of the stranger, that hath joined
himself to the LORD, speak, saying, The LORD hath

*utterly separated me from his people. . .I will give
them an everlasting name, that shall not be cut off.
Also the sons of the stranger, that join themselves to
the LORD, to serve him, and to love the name of the
LORD, to be his servants, every one that keepeth the
sabbath from polluting it, and taketh hold of my
covenant; even them will I bring to my holy
mountain, and make them joyful in my house of
prayer.* (Is. 56:3-7)

*Behold my servant, whom I uphold; mine elect, in
whom my soul delighteth; I have put my spirit upon
him: he shall bring forth judgment to the Gentiles.*
(Is. 42:1)

*And many nations shall be joined to the LORD in
that day, and shall be my people.* (Zech. 2:11)

*And in that day there shall be a root of Jesse, which
shall stand for an ensign of the people; to it shall the
Gentiles seek: and his rest shall be glorious.*
(Is. 11:10)

*So shall ye divide this land unto you according to
the tribes of Israel. And it shall come to pass, that ye
shall divide it by lot for an inheritance unto you,
and to the strangers that sojourn among you. . .and
they shall be unto you as born in the country among
the children of Israel; they shall have inheritance
with you among the tribes of Israel.* (Ezek. 47:21-22)

It is to the Messiah that Moses and the other prophets bear witness. Specific details about the Messiah were written in the prophets so that He might be recognized when He came.

The prophets spoke of His birth: The Messiah would be born a male child (Is. 9:6), He would be born of the seed of woman [not the seed of man] (Gen. 3:15), there would be something outstanding about the conception of the young woman who would bear Him that would make His unusual birth a sign

(Is. 7:14), He would be a descendant of Abraham, Isaac, Jacob, Judah and David (Gen. 22:18;21:12; 28:14; 49:10; Jer. 23:5; Is. 11:1), He would be born in Bethlehem of Judah (Micah 5:2). He would come before the destruction of the Second Temple (Dan. 9:26).

The prophets spoke of the Messiah's ministry: He would be preceded by a messenger (Mal. 4:5,6), He would be a prophet like Moses (Deut. 18:17-19), He would be anointed with God's Spirit and there would be power in His righteous words (Is. 11:1-5; 42:1; 61:1-3), He would be meek, gentle and compassionate (Is. 42:2-3), He·would be rejected by the religious leaders (Ps. 118:22), He would present Himself as King, lowly riding upon an ass (Zech. 9:9).

They wrote about His death and resurrection: He would be rejected, forsaken and left alone (Is. 63:3), rulers would plot together against him (Ps. 2:1-3), He would be hit on the cheek and spit upon (Micah 5:1; Is. 50:6), He would be killed (Zech. 13:7, Is. 53:12), He would not protest His death (Is. 53:7), He would be pierced (Zech. 12:10), He would die with transgressors (Is. 53:12), He would intercede for the transgressors (Is. 53:12), He would be buried in a rich man's grave (Is. 53:9), He would not stay dead (Is. 53:10,11).

Passover In Israel's Restoration

The irregular passover spoken of by the prophet Ezekiel (Ezek. 45:21-24) is set in his prophecies about future restoration of Israel under Messiah the Prince (ch. 33-48). In these prophecies, Messiah the Prince, the Son of David will reign, establishing the covenant of peace and giving the people a new heart. (Ezek. 34,36) Ezekiel's details about passover week sacrifices do not jibe with the Law. Considering Ezekiel's symbolic language, it is probable that the prophecy of the restored Temple and its service, including passover, should be taken symbolically. The number seven perhaps speaks of God's own Perfect Sacrifice, Messiah the Prince's offering.

Shortly after his prophecy about the future passover, Ezekiel speaks of a symbolic river of life coming from the temple of God with life-giving trees growing along its banks (Ezek. 47:7-12). These eternal trees with an inexhaustable supply of fruit, reminiscent of the tree of life lost in Eden, are for sustenance and healing in the land of Israel —belonging in the future not only to Israel's blood descendants but also to strangers who will share in the inheritance of God's chosen (Ezek. 47:21-23).

6

IN REMEMBRANCE OF ME

*For I received of the Lord that which also I delivered
unto you, That the Lord Jesus the same night in
which He was betrayed took bread: And when he
had given thanks, he brake it, and said, Take, eat:
this is my body, which is for you: this do in
remembrance of me. After the same manner also he
took the cup, when he had supped, saying, This cup
is the new testament in my blood: this do ye, as oft
as ye drink it, in remembrance of me.*

(I Cor. 11:23-25)

At Jesus' last supper with His disciples—a Passover meal,
He instituted a simple but profoundly-meaningful ceremony
which symbolized the fulfillment in His sacrifice not only of
Passover, but also of the Law's entire sacrifice system. He
instructed His disciples to ritually eat unleavened bread and
drink wine in remembrance of His body and blood given for
them:

*And as they were eating, Jesus took bread, and
blessed it, and brake it, and gave it to the disciples,
and said, Take eat; this is my body. And he took the
cup, and gave thanks, and gave it to them, saying,
Drink ye all of it; For this is my blood of the new
testament, which is shed for many for the remission
of sins. But I say unto you, I will not drink
henceforth of this fruit of the vine, until that day
when I drink it new with you in my Father's
kingdom.* *(Matt. 26:26-29)*

*And as they did eat, Jesus took bread, and blessed,
and brake it, and gave to them, and said, Take, eat:*

69

this is my body. And he took the cup, and when he had given thanks, he gave it to them: and they all drank of it. And he said unto them, This is my blood of the new testament, which is shed for many. Verily I say unto you, I will drink no more of the fruit of the vine, until that day that I drink it new in the kingdom of God. (Mk. 14:22-25)

And he said unto them, With desire I have desired to eat this passover with you before I suffer: For I say unto you, I will not any more eat thereof, until it be fulfilled in the kingdom of God. And he took the cup, and gave thanks, and said, Take this, and divide it among yourselves: For I say unto you, I will not drink of the fruit of the vine, until the kingdom of God shall come. And he took bread, and gave thanks, and brake it, and gave unto them, saying, This is my body which is given for you: this do in remembrance of me. Likewise also the cup after supper, saying, This cup is the new testament in my blood, which is shed for you. (Lk. 22:15-20)

The Lord Jesus the same night in which He was betrayed took bread: And when he had given thanks, he brake it, and said, Take, eat: this is my body, which is for you: this do in remembrance of me. After the same manner also he took the cup, when he had supped, saying, This cup is the new testament in my blood: this do ye, as oft as ye drink it, in remembrance of me. (I Cor. 11:23-25)

This Do In Remembrance Of Me

The ceremony Jesus instituted to show forth His death was not the Passover meal of the Law. He excluded two of the three mandatory Passover foods and included one never designated in the Law. Instead of the passover lamb, unleavened bread, and bitter herbs, Jesus told His disciples to eat unleavened bread and drink wine in remembrance of Him.

Jesus was clearly referring to sacrifice when He said the bread represented His body given and the wine His blood poured out for the remission of sins. Meal offerings, actually unleavened bread (Lev. 2:1-12), and wine were offered with the daily, Sabbath, and other sacrifices. The meal offering was offered on the altar with the lambs at the morning, evening, and Sabbath sacrifices on behalf of the nation. Wine, the drink offering accompanying these sacrifices, was poured out in the holy place (Nu. 28:7). Similarly, meal and wine were offered with the Firstfruits and Shavuot (Pentecost) offerings and peace offerings.

However, while the meal and wine were offered with many sacrifices, they were not offered with the Passover sacrifice or with any of the sacrifices of the week of Unleavened Bread (although unleavened bread, by Law, and wine, by custom, were **eaten** with the Passover sacrifice.) So, while Jesus instituted the "Lord's Supper" at a Passover meal, and certainly had the Passover sacrifice in view as part of what His supper spoke of, He was indicating that His death fulfilled, and His Supper commemorated, other sacrifices, too. Passover alone did not fully prefigure His redemption. Jesus' redeeming and atoning death fulfilled every sacrifice of the law.

A few hours after instituting the bread and wine memorial, Jesus gave His life on the cross, fulfilling and forever ending all animal sacrifice. When he was crucified, Jesus hung on the cross at the time of the daily evening offering, but not at the time of the Passover sacrifice which had occurred the day before. Within a few decades, God allowed the destruction of the Temple where the sacrifices were offered.

The Lord revealed the theology of Jesus' sacrifice to the Apostles—in particular detail to the highly-educated Rabbi Saul

(Paul). The Apostles taught it and wrote it down. No more were God's people to kill and eat a passover lamb or any other sacrifice animal. Gone for God's people was a ceremonial meal of lamb.

Gone also for God's people were the bitter herbs. No Scripture commentary is given concerning this. In place of the bitter herbs Jesus gave a cup of life and joy.

This *Do* In Remembrance Of Me

Jesus instructed His disciples to "do [and continue doing] this." The Gospels do not record any specific teaching Jesus might have given about how often to eat the ritual meal He instituted. Paul's word to the Corinthians, which he had probably received from the other Apostles who had been with Jesus, was "as often as" or "whenever" you eat and drink it (I Cor. 11:25-26). Both of Paul's expressions of frequency could be interpreted to mean "whenever you celebrate this annual Passover feast as Jesus has revised it" or "however often you do this." No clear directions are anywhere given. Unlike the highly-regulated Old Testament Passover, the Lord's Supper is conspicuous for its lack of regulations.

This Do *In Remembrance* Of Me

The observance of bread and wine which Jesus instituted was a memorial. It was a way of telling His death in a symbolic way. The simple elements' would call to remembrance all that they symbolized and all that Jesus taught concerning them. Given in the context of a Passover meal—a ceremony in which the participants retold the Egypt deliverance with the aid of food symbols, the Lord's Supper was clearly intended to have a similar function. The disciples would have understood Jesus' symbolic teaching when He said "this is my body . . . this is my blood."

A little wooden cross for each follower of Jesus would have been sufficient as a reminder of a single event—His crucifixion at Calvary. But Jesus gave **bread and wine** as symbols of His sacrifice, intending His disciples to remember His death not as one isolated event, but in the context of **all** God's revelation; His death fulfilled the Law's sacrifices. He did not come to do away with The Law, but to fulfill it. The Law was to be remembered to better understand that which fulfilled it.

This Do In Remembrance *Of Me*

"Remember not the former things," God said through the prophet. Yet it was He who had commanded His people to commemorate Passover "forever." Jesus said, "Think not that I am come to destroy the law, or the prophets: I am not come to destroy but to fulfil" (Matt. 5:17). Jesus put all those teachings together for His disciples with the ceremony of bread and wine. "Remember **me**," He said.

Jesus said that Passover's commemoration of redemption in Egypt was no longer to be the focus of the mind and heart. The new focus was redemption from sin and death through the Messiah— the Deliverer and the Lamb. "Do this in remembrance of **me**."

To remember Jesus was to recall also the centuries of legal ritual He fulfilled—all the feasts, sacrifices, ceremonies, religious offices, and objects of worship. In place of the numerous complicated institutions of the Law, Jesus gave just a simple meal of two elements But these two "simple" elements spoke volumes about His person and work. They spoke of His fulfilling all that the Law, as well as the prophets, had foretold about Him.

The Bread

"This is my body [given] for you," Jesus said. (The best manuscripts do not say "broken for you." Not a bone of Him was broken in fulfillment of Passover imagery and other prophecy.) "Take ye and eat."

When Jesus designated the unleavened bread as a symbol of Himself, His disciples certainly recalled His previous symbolic teachings about bread. Their minds undoubtedly went back to the time around Passover of the previous year, 29 A.D., when Jesus fed the 5,000 (Matt. 14:13-21; Mk. 6:30-44; Lk. 9:10-17; Jn. 6:1-15), gave His discourse on the Bread of Life (Jn. 6:22-71), warned about the "leaven of the Pharisees and Sadducees" (Matt. 16:6-12; Mk. 8:14-21; Lk. 12:1) and "gave some bread crumbs" to the Gentile Syro-Phoenician woman (Matt. 15:21-28; Mk. 7:24-30).

In His discourse on the Bread of Life (John 6) Jesus, resisting the multitude's intention to make Him King because He miraculously provided food for them, taught that spiritual food is more important than food for the body (vs. 26-27), that He Himself was the spiritual food come down from heaven which the manna typified (vs. 31-51), and that man must spiritually "eat Him" (vs. 51-63). He said man must eat His body and drink His blood (vs. 50-58) meaning partake of His words and Spirit which give life (vs. 62-63).

The Wine

If Jesus had not previously explained that eating His flesh and drinking His blood meant to partake of His life by His word and His Spirit (Jn. 6:63), His disciples might have been horrified and repulsed by even the symbolism of drinking His blood. God in the Law had utterly forbidden eating or drinking blood:

> *And whatsoever man there be of the house of Israel, or of the strangers that sojourn among you, that eateth any manner of blood; I will even set my face against that soul that eateth blood, and will cut him off from among his people. For the life of the flesh is in the blood: and I have given it to you upon the*

altar to make an atonement for your souls: for it is
the blood that maketh an atonement for the soul.
(Lev. 17:10,11)

Be sure that thou eat not the blood: for the blood is
the life: and thou mayest not eat the life with
the flesh. *(Deut. 12:23)*

But Jesus, now teaching that He fulfilled all the typology of animal sacrifice, said to symbolically drink **His** blood shed for the soul's atonement. He said to partake of **His** life.

The blood of sacrifices poured out at the altar and the wine offerings poured out in the holy place were brought together in the cup Jesus ordained for His disciples to drink in showing forth His death. The blood of the Passover lamb put on the doors of the houses and later poured out at the altar at the door of the house of worship merged with the blood of other sacrifices in the symbolism of the Last Supper's cup. The blood and wine of sacrifice foretold and represented Jesus' blood poured out for sin.

Jesus' words, "the new covenant in my blood" would have reminded His disciples of the passage about the "blood of the covenant" in the Law (Ex. 24). The Lord called Moses, Aaron, Nadab, Abibu and 70 elders of Israel up to the Mountain of Sinai. There they built an altar and sacrificed burnt offerings and peace offerings to Him. Moses took half the sacrifice blood and sprinkled it on the altar. Then he read the book of the covenant to the people. They agreed to keep it, whereupon Moses took the other half of the blood and sprinkled it on the people saying, "Behold the blood of the covenant, which the Lord hath made with you concerning all these words" (Ex. 24:8). Then Moses, Aaron, Nadab, Abihu and the 70 elders went up into the mountain, saw God, and ate and drank in His presence (Ex. 24:11). God called Moses farther up the mountain to meet with Him and receive from Him the covenant (which God had already given Moses, and Moses had written in a book) written by God's own hand upon tables of stone (24:12).

The new covenant in Jesus' blood was the eternal covenant spoken of by the prophets—the covenant of peace with God, of forgiveness of sin by God's mercy, of cleansing from sin, and of God's imputed righteousness (Jer. 31:31-34; Is. 54:8-17; 55:1-3; Ezek. 37:23-26). The words of this covenant were sealed with the blood of Jesus. Those eating and drinking the food of the new covenant were to abide in Jesus' life—in His Word, in His love (John 14-16). He would pour upon them His Spirit who would write God's law of love on the tables of their hearts.

The ritual of bread and wine undoubtedly also reminded the disciples of the Sabbath feast of God and man in the Tabernacle's holy place. There on the Sabbath the priests ate before the Lord the unleavened shewbread cakes, the pierced bread of God's presence. There in the holy place the Lord received the wine of the Sabbath offering poured out to Him (Nu. 28:7-9). Jesus offered to all His followers the food of the priests and of the Lord: "Take eat...drink, all of you, of it."

Just as His institution of bread and wine vitally changed the Passover commemoration, so Jesus prophesied still another change to come in the Eternal Feast of Redemption. The bread and wine was to be eaten by His disciples, apart from His physical presence, for a time only. A day was coming in which He and His disciples would together drink the fruit of the vine new in the Kingdom of God (Matt. 26:29; Mk. 14:25).

7

CHRIST OUR PASSOVER

For even Christ our Passover is sacrificed for us.
(I Cor. 5:7)

The contemporaries of Jesus who accepted Him as Messiah applied Passover imagery and prophecy to Him. To them, Jesus the Messiah fulfilled the Passover of the Law.

On Palm Sunday crowds of Passover pilgrims ascribed to Jesus the Messianic fulfillment of Psalm 118—one of the Passover psalms from the Hallel. They subsequently stumbled over the fact that He did not immediately take political power and deliver them from Roman rule according to their hopes and expectations, that He instead was crucified. But after He rose from the dead and pointed out how the prophets said the Messiah must suffer, their eyes were opened and they understood and accepted the fact that Messiah was not only a prophet and deliverer like Moses, but also a sacrifice like the passover lamb. The Epistles give voice to this Christian theology.

Messiah The King

Jesus presented Himself to the nation of Israel as Messiah and King as He entered Jerusalem for Passover 30 A.D. riding upon an ass and upon a colt, the foal of the ass, in fulfillment of Zechariah's prophecy (Zech. 9:9; Matt. 21:1-11; Mk. 11:1-11; Lk. 19:29-44; Jn. 12:12-19). A great multitude of the people accepted the validity of His act—so many that the unaccepting Pharisees lamented, ''Lo, the world is gone after him! (Jn. 12:19).

The people would not have accepted Jesus as Messiah if He

had merely ridden into Jerusalem on a donkey trying to foist upon them a belief that He fulfilled Zechariah's prophecy when there were no other reasons to believe He fulfilled it. They so readily accepted Him because He fulfilled other prophecy, because John the Baptist had witnessed that He was of God, because His teachings were with authority and power in the Spirit of God, and because he performed mighty miracles to confirm His word (the most recent being the raising of Lazarus who had been dead 4 days.). The first believers accepted Him because John the Baptist had said He was sent from God, and because He fulfilled the specific prophecies about Messiah. They testified, "We have found Him of whom Moses in the Law and also the Prophets wrote" (Jn. 1:45). Jesus' teaching and miracles confirmed to them that He was indeed the Messiah. Popular acceptance of Jesus by the Jewish people was so widespread that the politically-concerned chief priests and Pharisees came together in council to plan His death saying, "If we let him thus alone, all will believe on him, and the Romans shall come and take away both our place and nation." (Jn. 11:47-48).

When He presented Himself as Messiah-King, the people accepted His claim and ascribed to Him the Messianic fulfillment of Psalm 118. This Psalm from the Hallel was one of those sung by the Levites every year at Passover as they sacrificed the passover lambs in the Temple. It was considered to have been written by Moses. The second half of the Psalm says:

> The LORD is my strength and song, and is become my salvation. The voice of rejoicing and salvation is in the tabernacles of the righteous: the right hand of the LORD is exalted: the right hand of the LORD doeth valiantly. I shall not die, but live, and declare the works of the LORD. The LORD hath chastened me sore: but he hath not given me over unto death.
>
> Open to me the gates of righteousness: I will go into

them, and I will praise the LORD: This gate of the LORD, into which the rightous shall enter. I will praise thee: for thou hast heard me, and art become my salvation.

The stone which the builders refused is become the head stone of the corner. This is the LORD's doing; it is marvelous in our eyes. This is the day which the LORD hath made; we will rejoice and be glad in it.

Save now [Hosanna], I beseech thee, O LORD; O LORD, I beseech thee, send now prosperity.

Blessed by he that cometh in the name of the LORD: we have blessed you out of the house of the LORD.

God is the LORD, which hath shewed us light: bind the [festal] sacrifice with cords, even unto the horns of the altar [order a festival procession with shady branches even to the horns of the altar].

Thou art my God, and I will praise thee: thou art my God, I will exalt thee. O give thanks unto the LORD; for he is good: for his mercy endureth for ever.
(Ps. 118:14-29)

"Hosanna [save now]," the Passover pilgrims cried out to Jesus as they formed a procession with branches in their hands. "Save now, Son of David [Messiah]; blessed is he, the King, that cometh in the name of the Lord: blessed is the kingdom that cometh, the kingdom of our father David; peace in Heaven and glory in the highest" (Matt. 21:8-9; Mk. 11:8-10; Lk. 19:36-38; Jn. 12:12-13).

Inside the city of Jerusalem, the procession of people proclaimed Jesus to be "**the** prophet" (Matt. 21:10)—possibly the definitive article signifying their belief that Jesus was that "prophet like myself" which Moses had foretold (Deut. 18:18)—a belief many had earlier clearly expressed (Jn. 6:14; 7:40) and others would later express (Acts 3:22-23; 7:37).

When some Pharisees told Jesus to rebuke His disciples for the titles and praise they were giving Him, He answered that if the people did not so praise Him, the stones of the ground would (Lk. 19:39-40).

A day or two later Jesus took other words from Psalm 118 and applied them to Himself and to the religious leader's rejection of Him:

> *Jesus saith unto them [the chief priests, scribes and elders], "Have ye never read in the scriptures, 'The stone which the builders rejected, the same was made the head of the corner: This was from the LORD, and it is marvellous in our eyes'?*
>
> *And when the chief priests and Pharisees heard his parables, they perceived that he spake of them. (Matt. 21:42-46; Mk. 12:10-12; Lk. 20:17-19 quoting Ps. 118:22).*

Earlier Jesus had quoted Psalm 118:26 predicting the religious leaders' rejection of Him:

> *O Jerusalem, Jerusalem, which killest the prophets, and stonest them that are sent unto thee; how often would I have gathered thy children together, as a hen doth gather her brood under her wings, and ye would not! Behold, your house is left unto you desolate: and verily I say unto you. Ye shall not see me, until the time come when ye shall say, 'Blessed is he that cometh in the name of the LORD'.*

Later, the Apostles Peter and Paul, looking back on Palm Sunday and the events following during Passover week, discussed Psalm 118:22 as referring to Jesus, who the religious leaders rejected. He who the religious leaders rejected God made the Head of those who ratified the New Covenant. (Acts 4:11; I Pet. 2:6-8; Eph. 2:20).

Messiah The Sin Bearer

Jesus' followers were crushed when He was crucified. Their political hopes had been dashed: "We trusted that it had been he which should have redeemed Israel" (Lk. 24:21). But then the risen Messiah dealt with their confusion and depression that he had not at that time fulfilled the prophecies about His (still-future) political reign on earth. He told them they could not select parts of God's Word to believe; they had to take it all. The same prophets which spoke of Messiah's glorious reign also spoke of His suffering for sin. Jesus said to His disciples:

"O foolish men and slow of heart to believe in all that the prophets have spoken! Was it not necessary for the Messiah to suffer these things and to enter His glory?"

And beginning with Moses and all the prophets, He explained to them the things concerning Himself in all the Scriptures.   *(Luke 24:25-27)*

He said to them, "These are My words which I spoke to you while I was still with you, that all things which are written about Me in the Law of Moses and the Prophets and the Psalms must be fulfilled."

Then He opened their minds to understand the Scriptures, and He said to them, "Thus it is written, that the Christ should suffer and rise again from the dead the third day; and that repentance for forgiveness of sins should be proclaimed in His name to all the nations, beginning from Jerusalem."

(Luke 24:44-47)

Messiah Our Passover

John the Baptist was the forerunner of Messiah. Jesus had called him Elijah (Matt. 17:10-13; Mk. 9:11-13) in fulfillment of Malachi's prophecy (Mal 4:5). The Lord revealed to John that Jesus was "the Lamb of God which taketh away the sin of the world" (Jn. 1:29). The Lord also revealed to John that Jesus was the One who would pour out the Spirit as foretold by the prophets (Jn. 1:33).

And so it came to pass. Jesus was sacrificed as a lamb for sinners at Passover. He rose from the grave on the Passover Day of Firstfruits; He was the Firstfruits of the "kernal of grain which abided not alone but died and fell into the ground in order to produce more grain" (Jn. 12:24-36). During Pentecost, the harvest feast linked to Passover by the counting of 50 days (Lev. 23:5-21), Jesus poured out the Spirit of God upon His disciples—the earnest (pledge) of the eternal life He had obtained for them (II Cor. 5:5; Eph. 1:13-14).

Immediately after Pentecost, Jesus' disciples began to preach the Gospel of His death and resurrection for the remission of sins and reception of the Spirit and eternal life. The sermons recorded in Acts are filled with quotations from the prophets with comments on how Messiah Jesus fulfilled them. The Epistles expound the Gospel, including Jesus' fulfillment of Passover.

The Apostle Paul wrote only seven words about Messiah fulfilling the Passover sacrifice, but those seven words say much: "Christ our Passover is sacrificed for us" (I Cor. 5:7). Paul says Messiah (Christ) is the ultimate Passover for those who receive Him. He says Messiah was sacrificed, meaning His death was for others. The "our" and "us" in Paul' statement to the Corinthians were Jewish and Gentile believers.

Paul's theological statement treats the Passover of the Law not only as a commemoration of an important event in the history of the Jewish nation, but also as a picture of Messiah's coming sacrifice to redeem mankind from sin and death. In other New Testament passages, certain Old Covenant events and institutions are similarly considered pictures of New Covenant truths (see, for example, I Cor. 10:4,6,11; Col. 2:17; Heb. 7:15; 8:5; 10:1). The New Testament writers did not simply look back on Old Covenant institutions with hindsight and then call them pictures of things to come later. It had also been declared by the Lord in those Old Covenant days that He spoke through pictures looking ahead and speaking of things to come. (See Hos. 12:9-10).

Guided by the Spirit of God and His written revealed Word, the Apostles meditated on various details of Old Covenant Passover and saw how they were fulfilled by Christ. The Apostle John saw a fulfillment of Passover imagery (no bone of the passover lamb could be broken) in the fact that the soldiers at the crucifixion did not break Jesus' legs as they did the other victims' (Jn. 19:31-36). Paul picks up on Passover imagery of redemption when he says Christ's blood (like the passover lamb's blood) has redeemed and purchased the Church of God (Acts 20:28; Eph. 1:7; Col. 1:13-14). Peter and John likewise employ the imagery of redemption by the passover lamb's blood (I Pet. 1:18-20; Rev. 5:9).

Messiah The Firstfruits

When Paul said, "Now is Christ risen from the dead, and become the firstfruits of them that slept" (I Cor. 15:20), he was referring to Firstfruits Sunday of Passover week (Lev. 23:5-14), speaking figuratively about Messiah's resurrection. Christ's resurrection had not only fulfilled the symbolism, it had actually occurred historically on Firstfruits Sunday of Passover week 30 A.D. (Matt. 28:1-10; Mk. 16:1-11; Lk. 23:56-24:12; Jn. 20:1-18).

In teaching the Corinthians about resurrection, Paul also referred to Isaiah's prophecy about the "feast for all people" because of the destruction, in Jerusalem, of death (Is. 25:6-8; I Cor. 15). Because of Messiah's death and resurrection, all men shall rise from the grave. Then shall be the complete fulfillment of the prophecy, "Death is swallowed up in victory" (Is. 25:8; I Cor. 15:54).

Paul's teaching on resurrection discusses how death passed upon all men because of the sin in Eden, how God has provided redemption from sin and death in Messiah Jesus, the Sin Bearer Who rose victoriously from the grave and reigns in righteousness until He returns to earth in glory to put down all earthly power and restore all things to the Father:

> *Wherefore, as by one man sin entered into the world, and death by sin; and so death passed upon all men, for that all have sinned... For if by one man's offence death reigned by one; much more they which receive abundance of grace and of the gifts of righteousness shall reign in life by one, Jesus Christ. Therefore as by the offence of one judgment came upon all men to condemnation; even so by the righeousness of one the free gift came upon all men unto justification of life. For as by one man's disobedience many were made sinners, so by the obedience of one shall many be made righteousness. Moreover the law entered, that the offence might abound. But where sin abounded, grace did much more abound: That as sin hath reigned unto death, even so might grace reign through righteousness unto eternal life by Jesus Christ our Lord.*
>
> (Rom. 5:12, 17-21).

> *But now is Christ risen from the dead, and become the firstfruits of them that slept. For since by man came death, by man came also the resurrection of the dead. For as in Adam all die, even so in Christ shall all be made alive. But every man in his own order: Christ the firstfruits; afterward they that are Christ's at his coming.*
>
> *Then cometh the end, when he shall have delivered up the kingdom of God, even the Father; when he shall have put down all rule and all authority and power. For he must reign, till he hath put all enemies under his feet. The last enemy that shall be*

destroyed is death. For he hath put all things under his feet. But when he saith, all things are put under him, it is manifest that he is excepted, which did put all things under him. And when all things shall be subdued unto him, then shall the Son also himself be subject unto him that put all things under him, that God may be all in all. (I Cor. 15:20-28)

For this corruptible must put on incorruption, and this mortal must put on immortality. So when this corruptible shall have put on immortality, then shall be brought to pass the saying that is written, "Death is swallowed up in victory." O death, where is thy sting? O grave, where is thy victory? The sting of death is sin; and the strength of sin is the law. But thanks be to God, which giveth us the victory through our Lord Jesus Christ. (I Cor. 15:53-57)

8

LET US KEEP THE FEAST

*Therefore let us keep the feast, not with old leaven,
neither with the leaven of malice and wickedness; but
with the unleavened bread of sincerity and truth.*

(I Cor. 5:8)

Passover before Messiah involved a commemorative week
of greatly-regulated rituals. The Old Covenant Passover commemoration—that is, the ritual of the sacrifice, the ritual of
the passover meal, and the ritual of the week of Unleavened
Bread with its sacrifices and convocations, was observed
according to a myriad of strict rules governing every aspect
of the Feast. The New Testament writings present no such
Passover observance for Christians.

There are no rules there, as in the Law, telling the New
Covenant People of God to observe Old Covenant Passover,
and how to observe it. There are no accounts in Acts or the
Epistles, as there are in the books of Law and History, describing God's people observing Passover.

The Feast of Passover is not even mentioned in Acts and
the Epistles except twice in passing and once in figurative
language to make a spiritual application (Acts 12:1-6; 20:4-6;
I Cor. 5). Luke used Passover twice in Acts as a point of
reference for dating purposes. Paul spoke of the spiritual meaning of the Passover sacrifice and unleavened bread as he dealt
with the Corinthians about iniquity in their fellowship. None
of the three references to Passover contain information or
implications about observing the Old Covenant Feast, although
Paul's comments to the Corinthians confirm a theology that
Christ fulfilled Passover.

The lack of New Testament rules for, and descriptions of,

believers' Passover observance, of itself, could possibly imply an assumption by the early Jewish church that Passover was to be observed as usual—as it had been before Messiah. Or the lack of New Testament rules, of itself, could possibly indicate that the early church, after Christ's sacrifice no longer observed Old Covenant Passover (and other Old Covenant ceremonies). Since no specific teaching about Passover commemoration is given in the New Testament, one must consult Scripture in general, and any other available historic documents, for light on what the early Christians did specifically with Passover (and certain other Old Covenant institutions) for which God had commanded perpetual observance.

Some of the Scripture passages which pertain to such a study are Paul's teaching on the Lord's Supper (I Cor. 10-11), the "breaking of bread" passages (Acts 2:42, 46; 20:11), references to other feasts (Acts 20:16; I Cor. 16:8), general teaching about holy days (Rom. 14:5-6, 17; Col 2:16-17), passages treating Old Testament institutions as foretelling New Testament realities (e.g., I Cor. 3:16-17; 10:4-11; Col. 2:16-17; Heb. 8:5; 9:9, 23; 10:1), passages dealing with incidents of controversy between Paul and legalists (Acts 15 & 21; Gal. 2), and teaching about the necessity of keeping the whole law if one believes he is bound by the Law (Rom. 2:25; Gal 5:3).

There are no documents beside the New Testament that tell anything about Passover or the Lord's Supper for the first 100 years of the church.

Extra-Biblical descriptions of meals related to worship begin with Justin Martyr in 150 A.D. and the *Didache* of the second century or later. These were frequent meals which would not have been annual Passover meals. Early church historians, such as Eusebius (c.260-c.339) who had access to sources now destroyed, record that the early church had an annual commemoration of Jesus' death and resurrection which they called by such names as "The Lord's Passover," "The Christian

Passover," or "Pascha." (This annual commemoration later became "Easter.") This was not the Passover of the Law, but it was celebrated during the Passover season and commemorated how Christ fulfilled Passover. The Apostles John and Philip (according to John's disciple, Polycarp) held this annual commemoration on 14th Nisan, the date of the Passover sacrifice. Others held this annual commemoration on the Sunday after the 14th—the day on which Jesus arose. Some of the Gentile churches apparently had no annual commemoration of Christ's death and resurrection, but seemed to have celebrated only the more-frequent Lord's Supper. (See chapter 10 for extra-Biblical church history details.)

The Three Passover References

Passover 44 A.D. Luke mentions the Feast of Passover for dating purposes as he writes of Herod killing James and arresting Peter:

> *Now about that time Herod the king stretched forth his hands to vex certain of the church. And he killed James the brother of John with the sword. And because he saw it pleased the Jews, he proceeded further to take Peter also. (Then were the days of unleavened bread.) And when he had apprehended him, he put him in prison, and delivered him to four quaternions of soldiers to keep him, intending after Passover to bring him forth to the people. Peter therefore was kept in prison: but prayer was made without ceasing of the church unto God for him. And when Herod would have brought him forth, the same night Peter was sleeping between two soldiers, bound with two chains: and the keepers before the door kept the prison.*   *(Acts 12:1-6)*

Peter was arrested during "the days of unleavened bread" (vs. 3). He was freed from prison the night before Herod was going to bring him out to the Jews—presumably to kill him also (vs.6). This was at some point "after Passover" (vs. 4-6). The gathering at the house of Mary (vs. 12), to which Peter went after he was freed, was likewise "after Passover" and would not have been descriptive of any Passover week gathering of believers.

Passover 58 A.D. Paul and his co-workers Luke, Sopater, Aristarchus, Secundus, Gaius, Timothy, Tychicus, and Trophimus were not Passover pilgrims in Jerusalem for the Passover of April 58 A.D. Paul and Luke were at Philippi, and the others were at Troas:

> *And there accompanied him into Asia Sopater of Berea; and of the Thessalonians, Aristarchus and Secundus; and Gaius of Derbe, and Timotheus; and of Asia, Tychicus and Trophimus. These going before tarried for us at Troas. And we sailed away from Philippi after the days of unleavened bread, and came unto them to Troas in five days; where we abode seven days.* (Acts 20:4-6)

The mention of "the days of unleavened bread" seems to be a dating reference point. Nothing is said or implied about the believers observing the Old Covenant of Unleavened Bread. Nothing is said or implied about them commemorating the Feast in some new way. The passage **does** indicate that if they did commemorate Passover in any way, it was not according to the Law—at Jerusalem in community with Jews of the Old Covenant. Since the Temple had not yet been destroyed, all Jews abiding by the Law were bound to slay passover lambs and eat them at Jerusalem.

"Keep The Feast" Paul's comments about Passover and unleavened bread in his first epistle to the Corinthians (I Cor. 5) are an application of the Feast's spiritual significance to dealing with sin. His comments are set in the midst of his instructions about excommunicating a man committing iniquity. Paul likens excommunication to the purging of leaven during the observance of Unleavened Bread:

> *Your glorying is not good. Know ye not that a little leaven leaveneth the whole lump? Purge out therefore the old leaven, that ye may be a new lump, as ye are unleavened, For even Christ our passover is sacrificed for us: Therefore let us keep the feast, not with old leaven, neither with the leaven of malice and wickedness; but with the unleavened bread of sincerity and truth.* (I Cor. 5:6-8)

The Corinthian church included Gentiles (e.g., Justus, Acts 18:6-7) and Jews (e.g., Crispus, the chief ruler of the synagogue, Acts 18:8). The Gentile Justus worshipped God; his house joined closely to the synagogue. He would have observed Passover as a proselyte to the Jewish religion before he believed on Jesus. Gentiles in the Corinthian church had been educated about Passover, thus Paul assumes a familiarity with Passover on the part of both Jewish and Gentile Corinthians.

Paul's words, ''purge out therefore the old leaven, that ye may be a new lump, as ye are unleavened. For even Christ our passover is sacrificed for us'' (vs. 7), refer to purging out iniquity and walking the holy life of the Christian's calling. ''Keeping the feast'' is here taught as a holy lifestyle—for both Jews and Gentiles. Christ was the Passover for both Jews and Gentiles.

When Paul goes on to say, ''Therefore let us keep the feast, not with old leaven, neither with the leaven of malice and wickedness; but with the unleavened bread of sincerity and truth'' (vs. 8), it may be that he is adding some other thoughts, rather than merely repeating the previous exhortation. Because he speaks in the same sentence of both ''leaven of wickedness'' and ''old leaven'', ''old leaven'' might represent something other than iniquity in this second reference to it. Considering the emphasis in the next phrase on "truth," perhaps "old leaven" here refers to the legalism of the Old Covenant. The discussion about old leaven follows immediately upon Paul's saying, "Know ye not that a little leaven leaveneth the whole lump" (vs. 6)—the exact expression he used when writing to the Galatians about legalism versus faith (Gal. 5:9).

The Lord's Table And "Breaking Bread"

The Lord's Table. The bread and wine observance Jesus instituted at His last meal with His disciples, a Passover meal, represented the fulfillment of all Old Covenant institutions, not the Passover alone (see Chapter 6). Therefore, it is not equatable with Passover; it is not a New Covenant "Passover meal" since it symbolizes more than Passover alone symbolizes.

In discussing Communion, or the Lord's Table, in his first epistle to the Corinthians (I Cor. 10:14-28 and 11:17-34), Paul nowhere mentions Passover in connection with the bread and wine. Contrarily, he speaks of the communion observance as the spiritual counterpart of [all] the sacrifices (plural) of "Israel after the flesh" (I Cor. 10:18). Even in referring to the very night in which Jesus instituted the bread and wine, Paul makes no mention of it being Passover, but rather summarizes the evening as "the night in which He was betrayed" (I Cor. 11:23).

"Breaking Of Bread." Three New Testament references to "breaking bread" seem to refer to more than normal meals (Acts 2:42; Acts 2:46; Acts 20:7)—the first because it appears in a list which includes "the Apostles' doctrine" and "prayers," the second because it is mentioned in the same sentence with a description of "continuing daily with one accord in the Temple," and the third because it was what a group of believers did, in that instance at least, upon the "first [day] of the week" when they "came together."

These "breaking bread" passages do not speak of Passover or the week of Unleavened Bread. That, plus the fact that the breaking of bread seemed to be more frequent than yearly, seems to disqualify them as references to Passover observances.

Moreover, these passages do not use terms such as "Communion" or "The Lord's Table." For this and other reasons, they do not seem to refer to the Lord's Supper either. They do not speak of the cup. They do not speak of any memorial to Jesus' death. It would be expected that a reference to the Lord's Supper would mention the cup since Jesus gave more prominence to the wine than to the bread. Atonement is portrayed in the cup (Lev. 17:11; Matt. 26:28; Mk. 14:24; Lk. 22:20; I Cor. 11:25). The wine is prominent in the Lord's Supper as it will be partaken of anew in the future by Jesus with His disciples (Matt. 26:29; Mk. 14:25).

While these breaking bread references could possibly refer to Passover or to the Lord's Supper, it is not likely, for the reasons discussed, that they do. It is more plausible that they refer to what they seem at face value to refer to—daily fellowship around informal meals which involved discussion, teaching, exhortation, mutual encouragement and prayer. Blessings and prayers accompanied all Hebrew and Hebrew Christian meals, giving them a sanctity not experienced in pagan meals which were not acknowledged as a gift from God. Other references to breaking and blessing bread are Matt. 14:19; Mk. 6:41; Lk. 9:16; Jn. 6:11; Lk. 24:30, 35; Acts 20:11 and Acts 27:35.

Pentecost And "Holy Days"

Luke records an occasion where Paul made a special effort to be in Jerusalem on the day of Pentecost: " . . . for he hasted, if it were possible for him, to be at Jerusalem the day of Pentecost" (Acts 20:16). The record does not state why Paul wanted to be in Jerusalem on the day of Pentecost. A year earlier Paul said he planned to stay at Ephesus "until Pentecost" (I Cor. 16:8). This likewise does not state why he wanted to leave Ephesus at Pentecost; it does not say he would be going to Jerusalem. In the absence of any other input, it might be concluded Paul wanted to go to Jerusalem on Pentecost to celebrate the Feast.

There is, however, other input on how Paul viewed the feasts and what celebrating them meant to him. Both of these references to Pentecost are dated some 20 years after Paul's conversion and after he had written his epistles to the Galatians and Romans.

In his epistle to the Romans, Paul comments about the matter of esteeming certain days as holy above others—probably a reference to feast days, the Sabbath, and even Sunday—the day on which the Lord rose (Romans 14, especially verses 5-6). Paul seemed to personally consider all days alike. The Kingdom of God to Paul had to do not with religious ritual, holy days, and special foods, but with righteousness, peace and joy in the Spirit (vs. 17). There is a hint he would classify those Christians attached to days and ritual as among the "weak in faith" he speaks of (vs.1). But Paul's official teaching is that brothers who observe special days are no better or worse than those who do not. No Christian is to judge another in this matter. All must answer directly to God. There is liberty for the Christian who wants to celebrate certain days as special, there is liberty for the Christian who considers all days equally holy.

Four or five years later Paul warned the Colossians to resist those who tried to judge and pressure them "in meat, or in drink, or in respect of any holyday, or of the new moon, or of the sabbath" because those things are not the substance of Christianity; they were merely shadows of the reality to come in Christ (Col. 2:16-17).

Shadows Of Things To Come

Paul taught the Colossians that Old Covenant institutions

such as feast days were "a shadow of things to come"—shadows of the realities cast by the body which was Messiah (Col. 2:16-17). Shadows are not the substance, although they enhance the substance by helping to accent its depth and dimensions. Passover foreshadowed Messiah's redemption.

Paul taught the Corinthians that the spiritual redemption of those living in the shadows was the same as the spiritual redemption of those living later in the substance. The spiritual sustenance for the redeemed, whether in shadow or substance, is Messiah (I Cor. 10:4). In this teaching to the Corinthians, Paul also calls the events of the Exodus "types" for the Christian (10:6, 11).

The book of Hebrews elaborates on how Old Covenant institutions were prefigures of salvation in Christ (see, for example, 7:15; 8:5; 9:9, 23; 10:1). This view that Old Testament institutions speak figuratively of New Testament realities pervades the New Testament, and applies to Passover.

Paul And Legalists

The Jerusalem Council of about 50 A.D. (Acts 15) spoke to a dispute Paul and Barnabas had with certain men from Judea who taught that circumcision was necessary for salvation (vs. 1). In Jerusalem, certain believers of the Pharisees argued that circumcision was necessary, and so was keeping the law of Moses, which included the Old Covenant Passover sacrifice (vs. 5). The judgment and conclusion of the Council was that "through the grace of the Lord Jesus Christ we [Jew as well as Gentile] shall be saved" (vs. 11). Paul fully expressed his view that the works of the Law could save no one; only faith in Christ could save (Gal. 3, especially vs. 2, 11, 21, 24,25; also chapter 5). This is expressed also in Hebrews (7:19), possibly written by Paul.

While Paul (and Barnabas) "had no small dissension and disputation" with those who said circumcision was necessary for salvation (Acts 15:1-2), Paul did not so contend in another situation about 8-9 years later when the Jewish believers in Jerusalem convened again concerning his teaching (Acts 21:17-26).

In this situation, James and other elders of the Jerusalem church, after rejoicing over what God was accomplishing among the Gentiles through Paul's preaching, told him that "thousands" of Jewish believers there were "all zealous of the law." Moreover, those thousands of Jews had been told (possibly by agitating enemies of Paul) that Paul "teachest all the Jews which are among the Gentiles to forsake Moses, saying that they ought not to circumcise their children, neither to walk after the customs [including Passover]" (vs.21).

They asked Paul what his response to these charges were. They suggested a concrete thing he could do to prove to the Jews that he was not teaching Jews to forsake Moses. They suggested that Paul identify with some Jewish men who were about to participate in purification ceremonies at the end of a [Nazarite] vow by paying charges connected with that. Then the Jews could see that Paul "walkest orderly and keepest the law" (vs. 23-24). It stood as previously agreed that Gentiles had to observe no such thing (vs. 25). Paul consented, and did that.

Purification rites for a Nazarite vow did not involve sacrifice for atonement from sin, so Paul bent to keep peace with those who did not see things as he did. This was neither in hyprocrisy by the one who opposed Peter for hypocrisy (Gal. 2:11), nor in fear by the one who had fearlessly preached everywhere, and already endured much suffering for his faith. (Even while in the Temple concerning these men and the completion of their vow, Paul was apprehended by hostile Jews who beat him, intending to kill him (vs. 27-32).) Rather, this was Paul being "servant unto all. . . unto the Jews as a Jew that he might gain the Jews; to them under the Law, as under the Law, that he might gain them under the Law...to the weak as weak ...that by all means he might save some'' (I Cor. 9:19-22). This was Paul living out his teaching: ''Give none offence, neither to the Jews, nor to the Gentiles, nor to the church of God: Even as I please all men in all things, not seeking mine own profit, but the profit of many that they may be saved'' (I Cor. 10:32-33). ''Take heed lest by any means this liberty of yours become a stumbling block to them that are weak'' (I Cor. 8:9).

The same year as the Jerusalem Council, Paul (without pressure from others) had Timothy circumcised. Timothy's mother was a believing Jewess, but his father was a Greek, (an unbeliever?), and Paul considered Timothy's circumcision an expediency so that Timothy could travel with him (Acts 16:1-3).

Keeping The Whole Law

Paul firmly kept the teaching of Moses before those Jewish believers who insisted upon keeping customs of the Law with a sense of obligation:

> *Cursed be he that confirmeth not all the words of this law to do them. And all the people shall say, Amen.* (Deut.27:26)

Those who bind themselves to be keepers of the Law, must keep the **whole** law:

> *For I testify again to every man that is circumcised, that he is a debtor to do the **whole** law.* (Gal. 5:3)

> *For circumcision verily profiteth, **if** thou keep the law: but if thou be a breaker of the law, thy circumcision is made uncircumsion.* (Rom. 2:25)

James agreed with Paul on this point:

> *For whosoever shall keep the whole law, and yet offend in one point, he is guilty of all.* (Jas. 2:10)

Translated into commentary on keeping Passover according to the Law, this means that any Jewish believer who says he is obligated, because he is a Jew, to eat unleavened bread and bitter herbs must keep **all** the Law and also eat passover lamb. He must keep **all** the Law and eat **sacrificed** passover lamb — passover lamb sacrificed **at Jerusalem** and eaten there. He must, in community with all the Jews, also offer daily during the week of Unleavened Bread two flawless young bullocks, each with a meal offering of nine quarts of fine flour mixed with oil, one flawless ram with a meal offering of six quarts fine flour mixed with oil, seven flawless yearling lambs, each with a meal offering of three quarts of fine flour mixed with oil, and one male goat for a sin offering. He must not forget the daily offerings and the Sabbath offerings, etc. Of course, most of this is no longer possible. It has to be said: the Old is gone; the New has come.

9

MARRIAGE SUPPER OF THE LAMB

Blessed are they which are called unto the marriage supper of the Lamb. (Rev. 19:9)

In the book of Revelation Passover symbolism merges with other imagery to speak about things "which must shortly come to pass" (1:1). In the symbolism blending metaphors used previously in Scripture are still recognizable, so while Passover is not mentioned in Revelation, allusions to it are nevertheless discernible.

Elements of time also blend together in Revelation. The Eternal Lord, who sees past, present, and future in one view, gave the apocalyptic visions to the Apostle John while he was "in the Spirit" (1:10; 4:2; 17:3; 21:10), telling John to write of "things past, things present, and things yet to come" (1:19). Revelation is a view from God's side of eternity—a vision of His sovereign triumph over Satan and evil, over sin and death. God gave the messages of this book as an encouragement to His people still living within the bounds of time and space. Revelation is a more detailed version of "It is finished!" It is a word given to mortals still awaiting the final events of history which God sees as already accomplished.

There is a Lamb in Revelation, but He is not only the Passover Lamb, He is the Lamb of other sacrifice as well. He is a lamb slain, yet alive forevermore. He is the Lamb sacrificed at a certain point in human history, yet from God's viewpoint, slain from before the foundation of the world. Moreover, the Lamb is also the Lion of Judah. He is the Root of David, the Alpha and Omega, and much more.

There is a redeemed and delivered people in Revelation, but they are not only children of Israel, they are people from every nation and tribe of earth redeemed by the Lamb. They are called not "Israel," but "The Lamb's Bride," and the "New Jerusalem."

A "song of Moses" in Revelation is not only or even primarily the song Moses and the children of Israel sang at the Red Sea upon their deliverance from Egypt. It is the sobering song God gave Moses and told him to teach Israel as they were about to enter the Land of Promise. And it echoes one of David's Psalms. It is also called the Song of the Lamb. It is a spiritual song sung by saints of Old Covenant and New.

The eternal feast of redemption is not called Passover in Revelation. It is not called The Lord's Table either. However, it encompasses both of these. The feast in Revelation is called "The Marriage Supper of the Lamb."

The Lamb, the Redeemer-Deliverer, takes His people into a promised land. He takes them not to mere sod, but to the throne of God, to the fountain of living waters, to the tree of life in the paradise of God, to the New Heavens and New Earth.

The Lamb

Jesus Christ is the theme of Revelation. There He is spoken of 29 times as "the Lamb," with this reference to the Lamb appearing in half the chapters.

As God's Lamb, Jesus is the morning, evening, and Sabbath offering. He is the Sinbearer Lamb of which the prophet Isaiah writes, and of which Philip speaks to the Ethiopian in the book of Acts. He is the Lamb of God in the Gospel of John; the Redeemer Lamb in the first epistle of Peter. He is clearly the Passover Lamb of Exodus, for the Passover Lamb represents the **redemption** facet of salvation spoken of in Revelation:

> *And they sung a new song [to the Lamb] saying,*
> *Thou art worthy to take the book, and to open the*
> *seals thereof: for thou wast slain, and has redeemed*
> *us to God by thy blood.*   *(Rev. 5:8-9)*

The Lamb is the Redeemer of all mankind, fulfilling that redemption foreshadowed by the Passover in Egypt and foreseen by the prophets:

> . . .*for thou wast slain, and has redeemed us to God by thy blood out of every kindred, and tongue, and people, and nation.* (Rev. 5:9)

In Revelation Jesus is "the Lamb slain from the foundation of the world" (Rev. 13:8. See also I Pet. 1:18-20), although He suffered but once in point of time (Heb. 9:26). The Lord's eternal nature is clearly portrayed in the Apocalypse: He is called "Alpha and Omega," "the Beginning and Ending," "the First and the Last" (Rev. 1:8,11,17; 2:8; 21:6; 22:13). This is Jesus who in His incarnation declared, "Before Abraham was, I AM" (Jn. 8:58). Jesus, who is one with the Father (Jn. 10:30), is that Rock from whom the ancient Israelites drank upon their departure from Egypt (I Cor. 10:1-4), about whom Moses sang (Deut. 32).

Revelation's "Lamb slain" is also the Lion of Judah:

> . . . *behold, the Lion of the tribe of Judah, the root of David, hath prevailed to open the book, and to loose the seven seals thereof. And I beheld, and lo, in the midst of the throne and of the four beasts, and in the midst of the elders, stood a Lamb as it had been slain. . .* (Rev. 5:5-6)

The Lion of Judah, the Root of David, is the Messiah and Prince spoken of by all the prophets in their messages about the redemption which Israel (and the Gentiles with them) would experience in the Righteous One—the Sinbearer-King who would establish the eternal covenant.

Jesus is the Lamb slain, yet alive forevermore (1:18)—the Firstfruits of them that die and rise again (I Cor. 15). He is the Victor over sin and its consequences Who said, "I have the keys of hell and of death" (Rev. 1:18).

Jesus the Lamb shall return in glory to earth, coming in clouds, seen by all:

> *Behold, he cometh with clouds; and every eye shall see him, and they also which pierced him: and all kindreds of the earth shall wail because of him. Even so, Amen.   (Rev. 1:7. See also Zech. 12:10)*

At His return, the end will come when He will subdue all earthly kingdoms and power, putting all enemies, including death, under His feet. Then He will give the Kingdom over to the Father and will subject Himself to the Father who put all things under His feet "that God may be all in all" (I Cor. 15:20-28).

The Lamb who is one with the Father shall receive the eternal praise and worship of the redeemed:

> *. . . behold, a throne was set in heaven, and one sat on the throne. . . The four and twenty elders fall down before him that sat on the throne, and worship him that liveth for ever and ever, and cast their crowns before the throne, saying, Thou art worthy, O Lord, to receive glory and honour and power: for thou hast created all things, and for thy pleasure they are and were created.   (Rev. 4:2, 10-11)*

> *. . . and, lo, in the midst of the throne and of the four beasts, and in the midst of the elders stood a Lamb as it had been slain. . . And I beheld, and I heard the voice of many angels round about the throne and the beasts and the elders: and the number of them was ten thousand times ten thousand, and thousands of thousands: saying with a loud voice, Worthy is the Lamb that was slain to receive power, and riches, and wisdom, and strength, and honour, and glory, and blessing. And every creature which is in heaven, and on the earth, and under the earth, and such as are in the sea,*

> *and all that are in them, heard I saying, Blessing,*
> *and honour, and glory, and power, be unto him that*
> *sitteth upon the throne, and unto the Lamb for ever*
> *and ever. And the four beasts said, Amen. And the*
> *four and twenty elders fell down and worshipped*
> *him that liveth for ever and ever.*
>
> *(Rev. 5:6, 11-14)*

The Lamb's Bride

Jesus revealed to John that He would name His redeemed and delivered people a certain way:

> *Him that overcometh will I make a pillar in the*
> *temple of my God, and he shall go no more out: and*
> *I will write upon him the name of my God, and the*
> *name of the city of my God, which is new*
> *Jerusalem, which cometh down out of heaven from*
> *my God: and I will write upon him my new name.*
> *(Rev. 3:12. See also Is. 62:2)*

The city called "New Jerusalem" stands for more than buildings. It is a symbol of God's **people**, for it is also called the "Lamb's Bride":

> *And I John saw the holy city, new Jerusalem, com-*
> *ing down from God out of heaven, prepared as a*
> *bride adorned for her husband...And there came*
> *unto me one of the seven angels which had the seven*
> *vials full of the seven last plagues, and talked with*
> *me, saying, Come hither, I will shew thee the bride,*
> *the Lamb's wife. And he carried me away in the*
> *spirit to a great and high mountain, and shewed me*
> *that great city, the holy Jerusalem, descending out of*
> *heaven from God.   (Rev. 21:2, 9-10)*

The Lamb's bride is also called "Saints," who are arrayed in fine linen which stands for righteousness given them by the Lord:

*Let us be glad and rejoice, and give honour to him:
for the marriage of the Lamb is come, and his wife
hath made herself ready. And to her was granted
that she should be arrayed in fine linen, clean and
white: for the fine linen is the righteousness of
saints. And he saith unto me, Write, Blessed are
they which are called unto the marriage supper of
the Lamb. And he saith unto me, These are the true
sayings of God.*

(Rev. 19:7-9, See also 6:11 and 7:9, 13, 14)

This is the Jerusalem of God spoken of in the Epistles:

*For ye are not come unto the mount that might be
touched [Sinai]. . . But ye are come unto mount Sion,
and unto the city of the living God, the heavenly
Jerusalem, and to an innumerable company of
angels, to the general assembly and church of the
firstborn, which are written in heaven, and to God
the Judge of all, and to the spirits of just men made
perfect, and to Jesus the mediator of the new
covenant.*   *(Heb. 12:18-24)*

*Agar is Mount Sinai in Arabia and answereth to
Jerusalem which now is, and is in bondage with her
children. But Jerusalem which is above is free,
which is the mother of us all.*   *(Gal. 4:25-26)*

The Bride is Jewish: Symbolism about gates, foundations, a group of people numbering one hundred and forty-four thousand, and the remnant of a woman wearing a crown of twelve stars, speaks about the Jewish nature of the Bride of the Lamb.

The City of God, the New Jerusalem, has twelve gates. Each gate has the name of one of the twelve tribes of Israel upon it:

*. . . that great city, the holy Jerusalem. . . And had a
wall great and high, and had twelve gates, and at
the gates twelve angels, and names written thereon,*

> *which are the names of the twelve tribes of the*
> *children of Israel...*   *(Rev. 21:10-12)*

The gate of salvation is entered through the Jewish people—through the Jewish Messiah and the Word of God committed to the Jewish people. Jesus said, "Salvation is of the Jews" (Jn. 4:22). The prophet Isaiah had said of the New Jerusalem to which the Gentiles would flock that her walls would be called "Salvation" (Is. 60:18)

Jesus taught, "Think not that I am come to destroy the law, or the prophets: I am not come to destroy, but to fulfil" (Matt. 5:17). The Bride of the Lamb is that spiritual city "built upon the foundation of the [Jewish] apostles and [Jewish] prophets, Jesus Christ [the Jewish Messiah] being the chief corner stone" (Eph. 2:20):

> *And the wall of the city had twelve foundations, and*
> *in them the names of the twelve apostles of the*
> *Lamb.*   *(Rev. 21:14)*

Revelation's "hundred and forty-four thousand" who "have the Father's name" and "follow the Lamb" (7:3-8 and 14:1-4) are described as from the tribes of Israel—the "firstfruits of those redeemed from among men" (14:4). This symbolism may refer to other believers in addition to Jews since the "twelve tribes" named are not precisely the twelve tribes of Israel. (The tribe of Dan is omitted. Joseph is listed, and one of Joseph's sons, the half tribe of Manasseh is listed, while Joseph's other son, Ephraim, the other half tribe with Manasseh, is not listed.) Whatever is specifically meant by the symbolism of the hundred and forty-four thousand, a primary association with earthly Israel is clearly intended.

The woman wearing a crown of twelve stars of Revelation 12 is Israel who brought forth Jesus the Messiah anointed to rule the nations with a rod of iron, who has ascended to God in heaven (12:1-5). The "remnant of her seed, which keep the commandments of God, and have the testimony of Jesus Christ'' (12:17) are believers, the Bride of the Lamb.

The Bride of the Lamb is Jewish in spirit and in truth. She is not like those who, according to God's judgment, say they are Jews, but are not truly Jews. (Rev. 2:9; 3:9). As Paul put it:

> *For he is not a Jew, which is one outwardly; neither*
> *is that circumcision, which is outward in the flesh:*
> *but he is a Jew, which is one inwardly; and*
> *circumcision is that of the heart, in the spirit, and*
> *not in the letter; whose praise is not of men,*
> *but of God.*   *(Rom. 2:28-29)*

The Bride of the Lamb is truly Jewish because she receives God's revealed truth and follows the Lamb He sent (14:4)). She concurs with the Spirit of God (22:17) and is called "Jerusalem above which is free'' (Gal. 4:26). She stands in contrast to the body of those from the earthly Jerusalem, (I Cor. 10:18; Gal 4:25-26) who did not receive God's revelation but looked to the Law for salvation and thereby subjected themselves to bondage (because no one can keep the Law, and **keeping** the Law is necessary if the Law is to save) (Gal. 4:21;5:6; Heb. 12:18-20; Gal. 4:25).

The Bride Is Gentile: The people reedemed by the Lamb are not only racial descendants of Israel, they are people from every nationality of earth:

> *And they sung a new song, saying, Thou art worthy*
> *to take the book, and to open the seals thereof: for*
> *thou wast slain, and hast redeemed us to God by thy*
> *blood out of every kindred, and tongue, and people,*
> *and nation; and hast made us unto our God kings*
> *and priests: and we shall reign on the earth.*
>   *(Rev. 5:9-10)*
>
> *After this I beheld, and, lo, a great multitude, which*

> *no man could number, of all nations, and kindreds,*
> *and people, and tongues, stood before the throne,*
> *and before the Lamb, clothed with white robes, and*
> *palms in their hands...And one of the elders*
> *answered, saying unto me, What are these which are*
> *arrayed in white robes? and whence came they? And*
> *I said unto him, Sir, thou knowest. And he said to*
> *me, These are they which came out of great tribula-*
> *tion, and have washed their robes, and made them*
> *white in the blood of the Lamb.   (Rev. 7:9, 13-14)*

This fulfills the word of the Lord through the prophets that God's salvation and Holy Nation would one day extend fully to the Gentiles (e.g., Is. 11:10; 42:1; 56:3-7; Ezek. 47:21-22; Zech. 2:11. See also Rom. 15:8-12). It fulfills Jesus' word:

> *I lay down my life for the sheep. And other sheep I*
> *have, which are not of this fold: them also must I*
> *bring, and they shall hear my voice; and there shall*
> *be one fold, and one shepherd.   (Jn. 10:15-16)*

The One Fold: In Revelation the "one fold" Jesus spoke of is depicted as "twenty-four elders" (4:4, 10; 5:8-14; 11:16; 19:4), a symbolism incorporating both the Old Covenant's twelve tribes of Israel and the New Covenant's twelve apostles. The people of God are a unity of those obedient to God under the Mosaic covenant and those obedient to God under the covenant in Jesus' blood.

God's people are the flock of sheep chosen by Him before creation to inherit the Kingdom prepared for them "from the foundation of the world" (Matt. 25:31-34; Eph. 1:4; Rev. 17:8). They include lost sheep of Israel (Ezek. 34:1-16) and "other sheep" as well, with all being "one fold" and having the one Shepherd—Jesus (Jn. 10:16).

While the redeemed are from both Jewish and Gentile backgrounds, they are in essence one people in Christ

Rom. 3:27-29; Gal. 3:28; Col. 3:11). There is no difference between Jew and Gentile in God's sight (Acts 15:9; Rom. 3:22; 10:12; I Cor. 12:12-15; II Cor. 5:16-17; Gal. 6:15). He has no favorites (Gal. 2:6; Eph. 6:9; I Pet. 1:17). Together believing Jews and Gentiles are the chosen, the Holy Nation of kings and priests (I Pet. 2:9-10). Together they declare that Abraham is their father (Rom. 4:1-18) and Messiah Jesus is their Passover (I Cor. 5:7). Together they worship the Lord (Rev. 11:16; 19:4).

This unity of Jews and Gentiles in Messiah has always been in God's mind. It was His plan from the time of creation (Rev. 17:8; Eph. 1:4; Matt. 25:31-34). It was in His promise in Eden to bruise the head of the serpent that tempted the first man and woman into disobedience (Gen. 3:15). Before He made Israel His Holy Nation, God entered into covenant with Abram (an uncircumcised Canaanite and son of an idolater) and promised this man that through his seed He would bless all peoples of the earth (Gen. 12:3; 22:18). The subsequent establishment of the nation of Israel and the Law was a major part, but by no means the entirety, of God's plan to bring about His promised blessing. The Holy Nation, from its founding in Moses's day until Christ, always included a multitude of strangers grafted in to the children of Israel—a continuing token of things to come.

Israelites under the Mosaic Covenant knew their nation had never been a "pure race," but had always included others besides the blood descendants of Israel. But not until the great influx of Gentiles in the Apostolic era did it become clear that the God who loved Gentiles and Jews alike intended to fully give the Gentiles the type of blessings He had previously reserved for Israel. This inclusion of Gentiles in the Holy Nation was a mystery not well understood by ancient Israel, but clearly revealed after the coming of Messiah (Col. 1:26; Eph. 3:6; I Cor. 2:6-9; Eph. 1:9-10; Rev. 2:17; Mk. 4:11; Rom. 16:25-27; Rom. 11:13-24). It is in this unity that one can better understand Isaiah's prophecy that Israel, Egypt, and Assyria shall be a unity that will bless the land, and that Egypt, as well as Israel, shall be called "God's people" (Is. 19:24-25).

The Lord taught the essential unity of His people in the Passover. There was one rule for all, whether a blood descendant of Israel or a stranger. Not a bone of the lamb could be broken and not a bit of its meat carried from the place of eating in community. The blood descendants of Israel and the grafted-in strangers were one in this observance. After the Lord's Table was instituted, the unity of partakers was similarly stressed (I Cor. 10:16-17).

Unity in Love: Jesus prayed that His flock would be unified in love (Jn. 17:20-23). He knew there would be mental divisions, personality conflicts, and cultural clashes. He knew the potential for tension between Jewish and Gentile believers. In many ways, Jews and Gentiles were strangers to each other with their different backgrounds.

God had to command the children of Israel to "love the strangers as themselves," reminding them that they, too, had once been strangers to another people (Lev. 19:33-34).

When Jews came to Jesus asking Him to name the greatest command, He said, "Thou shalt love the LORD thy God with all thy heart, and with all thy soul, and with all thy mind." He added that there was a second command "like unto it," and quoted from Moses, "Thou shalt love thy neighbor [the stranger] as thyself." Jesus said that on those two commands "hang all the Law and the prophets." (Matt. 22:37-39 and Mk. 12:30-33, quoting Deut. 6:4-5 and Lev. 19:34. See also Rom. 13:8-10.) One scribe agreed, commenting that to keep those two commands "is more than all whole burnt offerings and sacrifices" (Mk. 12:33).

The Apostle John later elaborated on the way the second command is "like unto" the first: "He that loveth not, knoweth not God, for God is love" (I Jn. 4:8). He explained further,

"If any man say, 'I love God', and hateth his brother, he is a liar: for he that loveth not his brother whom he hath seen, how can he love God whom he hath not seen?" (I Jn. 4:20)

Song of Moses

Revelation has a song called "the song of Moses, the servant of God, and the song of the Lamb" (15:3). It says:

> Great and marvellous are thy works, Lord God
>   Almighty;
> just and true are thy ways, thou King of saints.
> Who shall not fear thee, O Lord, and glorify
>   thy name?
> for thou only art holy:
> for all nations shall come and worship before thee;
> for thy judgments are made manifest.
> (Rev. 15:3-4)

There are three songs of Moses in the Bible to which this passage could refer—the song Moses and the children of Israel sang at the Red Sea (Ex. 15), the song Moses taught Israel, at God's command, as they were about to enter Canaan (Deut. 31-32), and Psalm 90, attributed to Moses. (Psalms 113-118 may also be songs of Moses.) All of these songs speak of spiritual truths reiterated in Revelation, but the primary reference in Revelation 15 seems to be to the song in Deuteronomy, part of which correlates precisely with Revelation 15:3:

> . . . ascribe ye greatness unto our God. He is the
> Rock, his work is perfect: for all his ways are judg-
> ment: a God of truth and without iniquity, just and
> right is he. . . Rejoice, O ye nations, with his
> people. . .   (Deut. 32:3-4, 43)

In the song of Deuteronomy 32, the Eternal Lord is called Israel's "Rock"—a reference later applied to Jesus (I Cor. 10:1-4; Rom. 9:33; I Pet. 2:8).

The Song of Moses and the Lamb also seems to quote part of Psalm 86, a Psalm of David:

> *Among the gods there is none like unto thee, O LORD;*
> *neither are there any works like unto thy works.*
> *All nations whom thou hast made shall come and*
> *worship before thee, O LORD; and shall glorify thy*
> *name. For thou art great, and doest wondrous*
> *things: thou art God alone.*   *(Ps. 86:8-10)*

David's words in Psalm 86, together with the words in Revelation, are reminiscent of Moses's words at the Red Sea:

> *Who is like unto thee, O LORD, among the gods? Who*
> *is like thee, glorious in holiness, fearful in praises,*
> *doing wonders?. . . The people shall hear and*
> *be afraid.*   *(Ex. 15:11, 14)*

Other passages of Scripture come to mind in association with the last expression in Revelation's Song—that of God's righteous acts of judgment being revealed, or made manifest (e.g., Rev. 16:5-7; 19:2; Rom. 2:5). Many Scriptures speak generally of God's righteous judgment (e.g., Ps. 67:4; 96:10; Jer. 11:20; I Pet. 2:23). Revelation's plagues, which are part of God's righteous judgment, come before and after the Song of Moses and the Lamb. Some, but not all, of the plagues resemble the plagues God sent on Egypt through Moses: hail, darkness, rivers and seas turning to blood, sores on men. As the plagues are being poured out on earth, a "mighty angel" who stands upon the sea and upon the earth "lifts his hand to heaven and swares by him that liveth for ever and ever. " (Rev. 10:1, 5-6), echoing the song of Moses in Deuteronomy 32 about the Lord in the latter days judging Israel and the other nations with plagues and curses, and in the context of that judgment saying, "For I lift up my hand to heaven and say, I live for ever" (Deut. 32:40).

Judgment On Israel: The Song of Moses says that part of

God's righteous judgment in the earth was to deal with Israel who broke covenant with Him:

> *Of the Rock that begat thee thou art unmindful, and hast forgotten God that formed thee. And when the LORD saw it, he abhorred them, because of the provoking of his sons, and of his daughters. And he said, I will hide my face from them, I will see what their end shall be: for they are a very froward generation, children in whom is no faith.*
>
> *(Deut. 32:18-20)*

God's judgment against Israel, according to Moses and other prophets, would include cutting them off as His Holy Nation and making Gentiles the predominant part of those called His people:

> *They have moved me to jealousy with that which is not God; they have provoked me to anger with their vanities: and I will move them to jealousy with those which are not a people; I will provoke them to anger with a foolish nation.*
>
> *(Deut. 32:21. See also Rom. 10:19)*

> *But ye are they that forsake the Lord, that forget my holy mountain. . .therefore will I number you to the sword. . . Therefore thus saith the LORD God, Behold, my servants shall eat, but ye shall be hungry: behold, my servants shall drink, but ye shall be thirsty: behold, my servants shall rejoice, buy ye shall be ashamed: behold, my servants shall sing for joy of heart, but ye shall cry for sorrow of heart, and shall howl for vexation of spirit. And ye shall leave your name for a curse unto my chosen: for the LORD God shall slay thee, and call his servants by another name.*   *(Is. 65:11-15)*

Merciful Regathering: Moses prophesied that Israel would incur God's wrath with their disobedience and breaking covenant with Him, and would be scattered throughout the earth suffering many things. But the closing words of the Song of Moses are that God "will be merciful unto his land and to his people" (Deut. 32:43). Revelation says that Israel's latter-days sojourn in the wilderness, as it were, was to be only for a time (12:6,14). That time was "until the times of the Gentiles be fulfilled" (Lk. 21:24). There in the wilderness she would be nourished and protected through the persecution she would suffer (12:14-16), for Israel would not remain in that wilderness cut off from God, but God would regather the Israelites and they would return to Him:

> *And it shall come to pass, when all these things are*
> *come upon thee, the blessing and the curse, which I*
> *have set before thee, and thou shalt call them to*
> *mind among all the nations, whither the* LORD *thy*
> *God hath driven thee, and shalt return unto the*
> LORD *thy God, and shalt obey his voice according to*
> *all that I command thee this day, thou and thy*
> *children, with all thine heart, and with all thy soul;*
> *that then the* LORD *thy God will turn thy captivity,*
> *and have compassion upon thee, and will return*
> *and gather thee from all the nations, whither the*
> LORD *thy God hath scattered thee. . . and the* LORD
> *thy God will circumcise thine heart, and the heart of*
> *thy seed, to love the* LORD *thy God with all thine*
> *heart, and with all thy soul, that thou mayest live.*
> *(Deut. 30:1-6)*

> *For the Lord will have mèrcy on Jacob, and will yet*
> *choose Israel, and set them in their own land: and*
> *the strangers shall be joined with them, and they*
> *shall cleave to the house of Jacob.* *(Is. 14:1)*

The regathering of Israel would be after He had gathered Gentiles unto Himself. And then the Lord, the Bridegroom, would bring back into the Holy Nation the children of Israel who He had judged for unfaithfulness:

*Sing, O barren. . .for more are the children of the
desolate than the children of the married wife, saith
the LORD. Enlarge the place of thy tent. . .thy seed
shall inherit the Gentiles. . .thou shalt not remember
the reproach of thy widowhood any more. For thy
Maker is thine husband; the LORD of hosts is his
name; and thy Redeemer the Holy One of Israel; The
God of the whole earth shall he be called. . .For a
small moment have I forsaken thee; but with great
mercies will I gather thee. In a little wrath I hid my
face from thee for a moment; but with everlasting
kindness will I have mercy on thee, saith the LORD
thy Redeemer. . .behold, I will lay thy stones with
fair colours, and lay thy foundations with sapphires
. . .in righteousness shalt thou be established. . .This
is the heritage of the servants of the LORD, and their
righteousness is of me, saith the LORD.   (Is. 54)*

*For I would not, brethren, that ye should be ignorant
of this mystery, lest ye should be wise in your own
conceits; that blindness in part is happened to Israel,
until the fulness of the Gentiles be come in. And so all
Israel shall be saved: as it is written, 'There shall
come out of Sion the Deliverer, and shall turn away
ungodliness from Jacob: for this is my covenant unto
them, when I shall take away their sins. As concerning the gospel, they are enemies for your sakes: but as
touching the election, they are beloved for the fathers'
sakes. For the gifts and calling of God are without
repentance. For as ye in times past have not believed
God, yet have now obtained mercy through their
unbelief: even so have these also now not believed,
that through your mercy they also may obtain mercy.
For God hath concluded them all in unbelief, that he
might have mercy upon all.   (Rom. 11:25-32)*

The Faithful Remnant: Paul taught that God did not cut
off all of Israel when He grafted the New Testament Gentiles

into the Holy Nation. He did not cast away His people Israel — he cut off **some** of the unbelieving branches (Rom. 11:17), but there has always been a believing remnant which He has preserved and into which He grafted the Gentiles (Rom. 11:1-5,17). The Apostles and first Jewish believers were never cut off as part of the Holy Nation. The Olive Tree, God's Holy Nation, is at its roots and basic life God's faithful Israel with more Gentiles than ever included since the coming of Messiah, and of course now ratifying and keeping the New Covenant in Jesus.

Jewish people, the divinely-appointed guardians of the Word of God for centuries, are the more-natural branches of the Olive Tree into which Gentiles (the wild branches) have been grafted (Rom. 11:17-24) The receiving back into the Holy Nation of great numbers of Jewish people will be accomplished more naturally than bringing in of Gentiles, and it will bring immeasurable new life to the Body of Christ (Rom. 11:12,15)

Accordingly, the song in Revelation is the song of **Moses** and the Lamb. The Jewish nature of the Bride of the Lamb is preserved in Revelation, although the grafted-in redeemed people come from every nation and tribe of earth. God is keeping His promises to Israel of old. The Mosaic Covenant has been broken by the children of israel, but God has given a new and superior eternal covenant of salvation and peace. The eternal covenant embodies the Spirit of the Mosaic Covenant which is the Spirit of the Covenant of the Lamb. It is a covenant which Israel, and Gentiles with them, can and will keep in God's Son and in His Spirit.

The Marriage Feast

Just as the plagues God sent upon ancient Egypt had a ministry of inviting people to glorify the Sovereign Lord, so the plagues and cataclysmic events in Revelation invite people to repent from evil and glorify the Lord (Rev. 14:6-7). Many do not do so (9:20-21), but a remnant do (11:13). After the plagues, Revelation tells of a feast for those who have escaped God's judgment through the blood of the Lamb and have been delivered from the oppressing kingdom of the Evil One. This parallels the Passover in Egypt, but encompasses more than that symbolism covers. The Feast in Revelation is called the Marriage Supper of the Lamb:

> *And I heard as it were the voice of a great multitude, and as the voice of many waters, and as the voice of mighty thunderings, saying, Alleluia: for the Lord God omnipotent reigneth. Let us be glad and rejoice, and give honour to him: for the marriage of the Lamb is come, and his wife hath made herself ready. And to her was granted that she should be arrayed in fine linen, clean and white: for the fine linen is the righteousness of saints. And he saith unto me, Write, Blessed are they which are called unto the marriage supper of the Lamb. (Rev. 19:6-9)*

This is the Lord's feast prepared for all people (Is. 25:6), and blessed are those who have not refused to come (Rev. 19:9; Lk. 14:15-24). It is the feast of Passover truth unfolded and fully revealed—truth of an eternal nature (Ex. 12:14). It is the feast where Jesus and His Bride drink the wine of the Covenant in His blood new in the Kingdom (Matt. 26:29; Mk. 14:25).

The marriage metaphor of Revelation follows through on imagery the Lord had used previously to describe His relationship with His people. Israel is depicted by the prophets as a woman of no reputation whom the Lord found and betrothed to Himself. After the Lord married her and gave her His name and beauty, she became unfaithful to Him, and so merited His putting her away in justice and righteous wrath. But although Israel was unfaithful, God remained faithful. He promised to regather and restore Israel to Himself. (See Ezek. 16, Hosea 1-3, Is. 54 and 62, and Jer. 31:31-34):

Nevertheless I will remember my covenant with thee in the days of thy youth, and I will establish unto thee an everlasting covenant. (Ezek. 16:60)

For the children of Israel shall abide many days without a king, and without a prince, and without a sacrifice, and without an image, and without an ephod, and without teraphim: afterward shall the children of Israel return, and seek the LORD their God, and David their king; and shall fear the LORD and his goodness in the latter days. (Hos. 3:4-5)

For thy Maker is thine husband; the LORD of hosts is his name; and thy Redeemer the Holy One of Israel; The God of the whole earth shall he be called. . . For a small moment have I forsaken thee; but with great mercies will I gather thee. In a little wrath I hid my face from thee for a moment; but with everlasting kindness will I have mercy on thee, saith the LORD thy Redeemer. (Is. 54:5-8)

Thou shalt no more be termed Forsaken; neither shall thy land any more be termed Desolate: but thou shalt be called Hephzi-bah [My Delight is in Her] and thy land Beulah [Espoused]: for the LORD delighteth in thee, and thy land shall be married. For as a young man marrieth a virgin, so shall thy sons marry thee: and as the bridegoom rejoiceth over the bride, so shall thy God rejoice over thee.

(Is. 62:4-5)

God said that He would gather the Gentiles to Himself with Israel:

The LORD God which gathereth the outcasts of Israel saith, Yet will I gather others to him, beside those that are gathered to him.

(Is. 56:8. See also verses 3-7.)

The Gospels and Epistles speak of Christ as the Bridegroom

and the Church as the Bride (Matt. 9:14-17; 25:1-13; Mk. 2:18-20; Lk. 5:33-34; Jn. 3:29; II Cor. 11:2; Eph. 5:22-32).

The Lord betroths His Bride to Himself forever in righteousness, justice, love, compassion and faithfulness (Hos. 2:19-20). Just as of old, the New Jerusalem is beautiful because of **His** beauty:

> *And when I passed by thee. . . I said unto thee. . .*
> *Live!. . . and I spread my skirt over thee and covered*
> *thy nakedness. . . and entered into a covenant with*
> *thee, saith the LORD God, and thou becamest mine.*
> *Then I washed thee with water. . . and I anointed*
> *thee with oil. . . I clothed thee. . . I decked thee with*
> *ornaments. . . And thou wast exceeding beautiful,*
> *and thou didst prosper into a kingdom and thy*
> *renown went forth among the heathen for thy*
> *beauty: for it was perfect through* **my** *comeliness,*
> *which I had put upon thee, saith the LORD God.*
> *(Ezek. 16:1-14)*

While unfaithful Israel said her beauty was her own and "played the harlot" with the world, (Ezek. 16:15ff) faithful Israel says:

> *I will greatly rejoice in the LORD; my soul shall be*
> *joyful in my God; for he hath clothed me with the*
> *garments of salvation, he hath covered me with the*
> *robe of righteousness, as a bridegroom decketh*
> *himself with ornaments, and as a bride adorneth*
> *herself with her jewels.* *(Is. 61:10)*

> *Not by works of righteousness which we have done,*
> *but according to his mercy he saved us, by the*
> *washing of regeneration, and renewing of the Holy*
> *Spirit which he shed on us abundantly through*
> *Jesus Christ our Saviour; that being justified by his*
> *grace, we should be made heirs according to the hope*
> *of eternal life.* *(Titus 3:5-7)*

New Jerusalem's testimony would be that of people established in the Lord's righteousness, whose righteousness is of Him (Is. 54:14,17) and whose hearts are circumcised (Deut. 30:6). This is the teaching of the Apostles (e.g., Rom. 1-5). The Bride's righteousness is not her own, but is imputed by faith in David's Righteous Branch, the Messiah King who she calls "THE LORD OUR RIGHTEOUSNESS" (Jer. 23:5-6)

Return to Eden

The Lamb's Bride who is called the New Jerusalem, follows the Lamb through earth's tribulations. Then she feasts and rejoices with Him eternally in the new heavens and new earth (Rev. 21:1; Is. 65:17).

The Lamb will feed His Bride and take her to the living fountains of waters, and God will wipe away all her tears (Rev. 7:17). The living water is that about which Ezekiel wrote (Ezek. 47:1-12)—the fountain of water from the Temple which becomes a river on whose banks are trees of life:

> *And he shewed me a pure river of water of life,*
> *clear as crystal, proceeding out of the throne of God*
> *and of the Lamb. In the midst of the street of it, and*
> *on either side of the river, was there the tree of life,*
> *which bare twelve manner of fruits, and yielded her*
> *fruit every month: and the leaves of the trees were*
> *for the healing of nations.   (Rev. 22:1-2)*

This is the tree of eternal life which Jesus gives to His own (Rev. 2:7). It is the water of life which He gives (21:6) flowing "from the Temple" (which is God, for the Lord God Almighty and the Lamb are the Temple) (21:22):

> *And the Spirit and the bride say, Come. And let him*
> *that heareth say, Come. And let him that is athirst*
> *come. And whosoever will, let him take the water of*
> *life freely.   (Rev. 22:17)*

By His holy life, death and resurrection pictured in the

unleavened bread, the passover sacrifice and the firstfruits, Jesus has defeated sin and death. Revelation shows Satan bound (20:1-3), mankind resurrected (20:5,12-13), death, hell and unbelievers cast into the Lake of Fire (20:14), and believers partaking of the eternal feast of redemption. This is the word of the Lord through Isaiah at last come to pass:

> *And in this mountain shall the LORD of hosts make unto all people a feast of fat things, a feast of wines on the lees, of fat things full of marrow, of wines on the lees well refined. And he will destroy in this mountain the face of the covering cast over all people, and the vail that is spread over all nations. He will swallow up death in victory; and the LORD God will wipe away tears from off all faces; and the rebuke of his people shall he take away from off all the earth; for the LORD hath spoken it. And it shall be said in that day, Lo, this is our God; we have waited for him, and he will save us; this is the LORD; we have waited for him, we will be glad and rejoice in his salvation.* (Is. 25:6-9)

The Lamb's Bride, made holy in His righteousness, enters the eternal joy of the presence of God. She experiences Eden restored:

> *And there shall be no more curse: but the throne of God and of the Lamb shall be in it; and his servants shall serve him: And they shall see his face; and his name shall be in their foreheads.* (Rev. 22:3-4)

> *And God shall wipe away all tears from their eyes; and there shall be no more death, neither sorrow, nor crying, neither shall there be any more pain: for the former things are passed away. And he that sat upon the throne said, Behold, I make all things new. . . .And he said unto me, It is done. I am Alpha and Omega, the beginning and the end.* (Rev. 21:4-6)

10

THE PASCHA WAS CHRIST

And the blood of the Pascha, sprinkled on each man's doorpost and lintel, delivered those who were saved in Egypt, when the firstborn of the Egyptians were destroyed. For the Pascha was Christ who was afterwards sacrificed. . . . And as the blood of the Passover saved us who were in Egypt, so also the blood of Christ will deliver from death those who have believed. (Justin Martyr)

There are no documents besides the New Testament writings which discuss the Passover theology or describe the Passover-related worship of the church in its first 100 years. Historians must make educated guesses about what Passover meant to the church during the silent period between the time of the New Testament writings and that of the second, third, and fourth century documents in which reference is again made to Passover.

A perusal of 19th and 20th century history books yields a variety of conflicting pictures of that era. One can not even get certain answers directly from the statements of those ancient historians consulted by modern historians: Eusebius, 260-339 A.D.; Epiphanius, 315-403; Socrates, 380-439+; Theodoret, 393-460; Sozomen, mid 5th century.

The historian Josephus was a contemporary of the Apostles. He lived from 38-c.100 A.D.; But while Josephus says a few things about Jesus and John the Baptist, he makes only one brief reference to the active church of his day (the reference to Jewish persecution of the church under Festus). Some have thought that Josephus, being Jewish, did not write about the church because he was displeased or embarrassed that Jews had brought it forth. In Josephus's day the church was still under the leadership of the Jewish fathers, and many still viewed it as one sect of Judaism.

In the absence of clear documentation, any presentation of how Passover was observed in the first century must be considered open for discussion and challenge. This is also true concerning observance of the Lord's Table. The first reference, after the New Testament writings, to the bread and wine observance dates to approximately 155 A.D.

The Lord's Table

The Lord's Table, also called The Lord's Supper, Communion, and the Eucharist, was known to be rooted historically in Passover—Jesus instituted His supper at a Passover meal. It was recognized that the Lord's Table symbolism pertained to Passover, but not to Passover alone, for it symbolized Christ's death and resurrection as the fulfillment of all the sacrifices and feasts of the Mosaic Covenant. The Gospels, Epistles, Acts and other documents of the early church do not present any thinking that the Lord's Table was a ritual feast replacing Passover. It was not considered an "ongoing Passover observance" with new Christian perspective. It was something new and unique. It was celebrated not annually, as Passover had been, but more frequently—weekly for most believers (by most clear accounts). The ritual foods were the bread and wine, not Passover lamb, unleavened bread, and bitter herbs. In homilies related to the Lord's Table there is no indication that early believers considered it a revised Passover observance.

The first post-biblical reference to the bread and wine is in Jusitin Martyr's *First Apology*, c. 155 A.D. Justin makes no liturgical connection between Passover and Communion, and he might well have made such connection if he had seen any. Justin knew well the theology of Christ fulfilling Passover, and he expounded on that theology at great length in his writings.

The *Didache*, a document dated anywhere from the beginning of the second century to as late as the third century, has material which some historians and theologians believe refers to Communion. (Others believe this material does not refer to Communion.) But whatever the *Didache* is describing, it does not connect it to Passover.

Subsequent literature of the church similarly does not present the Lord's Table as being a Christian Passover observance.

The Annual Commemoration of Christ's Death

It seems that most, but not all, early Christians held an annual commemoration of Christ's death and resurrection which they **did** relate to the Old Covenant's annual feast of Passover. Apparently some all-Gentile groups at first had no annual observance whatsoever to commemorate Christ's death and resurrection; they observed only the more-frequent Lord's Table. But Jewish believers, Gentile believers who had been proselytes to Judaism, Gentiles in fellowship with Jewish believers, and perhaps some of the all-Gentile groups held an annual commemoration at the Passover season—the anniversary of Christ's crucifixion. This was in addition to observing the Lord's Table. Gentile churches which originally had had no annual commemoration began to adopt the custom of the others. Soon an annual commemoration was the custom of the great majority.

This annual commemoration was not the Passover of the Old Covenant. It was a celebration of how Christ fulfilled the Exodus Passover. The redemption in Egypt was remembered, but the focus was primarily on the greater redemption effected at Calvary by the Lamb of God. The commemoration built upon the Exodus event and was expressed in Passover imagery. Like the Old Testament Passover, the commemoration was a night feast. It was dated according to the Biblical lunar calendar, not the solar calendar adopted later.

Polycarp, a disciple of the Apostle John, who was also taught by Philip and other Apostles, so celebrated Passover. Irenaeus, who in his youth had studied under Polycarp, described him as a faithful and true leader of the church—one who had been instructed by the Apostles. Polycarp was appointed Bishop of Smyrna by the Apostles in Asia, and "always taught the things which he had learned from the Apostles, and which the church has handed down, and which alone are true."[1]

Melito, Bishop of Sardis (c.170 A.D.) observed Passover as fulfilled in Christ on the 14th Nisan. His "Homily on the Passion" begins with a Passover narrative from the book of Exodus. To Melito, Passover held a dual significance—first as a commemoration of the historical event in ancient Egypt, and second as a type of the sacrifice of Christ. Melito believed the slaying of the passover lamb pointed to Christ's crucifixion. The sparing of the firstborn by the passover's blood on the doors was a type of Christians being spared by the death of Christ.[2]

Many in Palestine and Asia Minor followed in this tradition. Their Passover observance, as judged by some later services, might have consisted of a Passover homily, a meal followed by the bread and wine observance instituted by Jesus, and singing of the Hallel (Psalms 113-118) and other hymns. New believers were baptized at this observance (as well as at other times, probably). The homily and hymns spoke of redemption in Messiah being a fulfillment of what the Exodus redemption prefigured.

Gentile groups evidently did not always view everything about this annual commemoration in the same way as the Jewish and Jewish-influenced groups did. Undoubtedly this was especially true with all-Gentile groups who adopted the annual commemoration without having a full knowledge of the Old Covenant Passover in which the annual commemoration was rooted.

There are no records of disagreement over the theology that

Christ fulfilled Passover typology. But there did develop a major conflict over the date on which to hold the annual commemoration. The Jewish-influenced groups held out for the 14th Nisan (the date the Lord had set as the permanent date on which to observe Passover), and the Gentile groups held out for the Sunday following the 14th Nisan (the day of the week on which Christ arose.)

Good Friday and Easter Sunday Once Called Passover

Before the annual commemoration of Christ's sacrifice came to be called Easter in some places, it was called by its original name, *Passover*. *Passover* is the anglicized form of *pascha*, which in turn is Greek for the Hebrew *pesach*. *Pesach* is the Old Testament word for the passover lamb and also for the Feast of Passover named after the passover lamb. *Pascha* is the Greek word used in the New Testament and other early writings to refer to four things—the Old Testament feast of Passover, the Old Testament passover lamb itself, the Christian festival of Christ's death and resurrection, and Christ the Paschal Lamb Himself. Before the introduction of the word Easter, some form of *Pascha*, or Passover, was used to refer to the Christian feast. It was called The Pasch, The Christian Passover, The Lord's Passover, Paschaltide, etc.

The early church named both Good Friday and Resurrection Sunday *Pasch*. Good Friday was called *Pasch Staurosimon* (Pasch of Crucifixion), and Resurrection Sunday was called *Pasch Anastasimon* (Pasch of Resurrection). The Eastern church still uses these names.

Passover remains the name in many countries for the church feast which English and German-speaking people now commonly call Easter. For example: Greece and Romania, *Pascha;* Italy, *Pasqua;* Spain and Portugal, *Pascua;* France, *Paque;* Norway, *Paskir* and Denmark, *Paaske*.

Passover Theology of the Early Church

The concept that Christ fulfilled the Old Testament Passover types and prophetic imagery was clearly understood in the early church. It was the theme of liturgy and song.

Justin Martyr (c. 100-165 A.D.) was a Greek Christian, one of Christianity's greatest apologists. His theology included the view that "the Lamb slain from the foundation of the world" was in fact the One whose blood saved the Israelites in Egypt. The Israelites' faith act of putting the lambs' blood on the lintels and doorposts looked forward to Christ's coming sacrifice. Although the Israelites in Egypt didn't yet understand it, the Eternal saw the blood of His Lamb on those doors.

When Justin wrote, "the blood of the Passover saved **us** who were in Egypt,"[3] he was verbalizing a theology which applied the past Egypt events to the Christian.

An ancient Vesper Hymn of the Paschal Festival reflects the theology of Passover held by early Christians:

> *The Lamb's high banquet we await*
> *In snow-white robes of royal state*
> *And now, the Red Sea's channel past,*
> *To Christ our Prince we sing at last.*
>
> *That Paschal Eve God's arm was bared,*
> *The devastating Angel spared:*
> *By strength of hand our hosts went free*
> *From Pharaoh's ruthless tyranny.*
>
> *O thou, from whom hell's monarch flies,*
> *O great, O very Sacrifice,*
> *Thy captive people are set free,*
> *And endless life restored in Thee.*

The Vesper Hymn was sung when believers were baptized. Since not only the Passover feast, but baptism as well, pictured the death and resurrection of Christ and the believer's redemption in Him, the early church united these two in a common ritual. Baptism was preferably administered on Easter night, at midnight—the hour when the LORD passed over the houses with the lambs' blood on their doors. A Paschal homily was given which compared the liberation of the believer from sin to the liberation in Exodus. This was followed by a meal and the observance of bread and wine which Jesus instituted, with prayers and the Hallel. (Psalms 113-118)

John of Damascus, in the eighth century applied Passover's symbolism to Christians. Two hymns from modern hymnals preserve his thoughts—*Come Ye Faithful, Raise the Strain* and *The Day of Resurrection:*

> *Come, ye faithful, raise the strain*
> *Of triumphant gladness,*
> *God hath brought His Israel*
> *Into joy from sadness.*
>
> *Loosed from Pharaoh's bitter yoke*
> *Jacob's sons and daughters,*
> *Led them with unmoistened foot*
> *Through the Red Sea Waters.*
> . . .
>
> *The day of resurrection,*
> *Earth tell it out abroad,*
> *The Passover of gladness,*
> *The Passover of God.*
>
> *From death to life eternal,*
> *From this world to the sky,*
> *Our Christ hath brought us over*
> *With hymns of victory.*

Nature of the Paschal Controversy

During the second and third centuries, the church became involved in what has come to be called *The Paschal Controversy.* A look at some of the documents from that era shows the entire Christian world in agreement that Christ fulfilled the Passover, but differing as to the day on which the annual

Christian Passover should be observed. This was no small controversy between a few extremists, but a world-wide church split involving the entire church.

In the beginning, Christians annually celebrated Christ's death and resurrection at the time of Passover in the month of Nisan, the actual anniversary of the Passion week events recorded in the Gospels. Epiphanius wrote:

> *So long at least as the first fifteen bishops of*
> *Jerusalem [those of Jewish descent] continued,*
> *the pascha was celebrated everywhere by all*
> *[Christians], or by a great majority of them,*
> *according to the lunar computation and method*
> *of the Jews.* [4]

There is no first century record of controversy about whether to hold The Christian Passover observance on the 14th Nisan or on the Sunday following. But by 120 A.D., such a controversy was underway, with the majority in the Jerusalem and other Asian churches holding their observance on the 14th Nisan (on whatever day of the week the 14th fell), and the majority in the Roman and other western churches holding their Christian Passover on the Sunday following 14th Nisan.

Early Handling of Differences

Under Sixtus, Bishop of Rome, about 120 A.D., the Romans and Asians in Rome were in conflict over this matter. Their disputation ended in agreement of mutual toleration of the differing customs.

When Polycarp, Bishop of Smyrna, visited Rome under Anicetus (155-166 A.D.), he and Anicetus differed regarding the day for celebrating the Christian Passover. Anicetus tried to persuade Polycarp to observe the festival on Sunday. But Polycarp, a disciple of the Apostle John, refused. He said that observance of Christian Passover on 14th Nisan had been the custom of John and the other Apostles with whom he had lived. Polycarp, in turn, tried to convert Anicetus to observe on the

14th, but Anicetus would not abandon the custom of the presbyters before him, of whose tradition he was. The two did not settle their differences, but parted in peace.

Intensification of the Controversy

The schism grew more acute under Soter (166-174 A.D.). By the time of Victor (189-199 A.D.), the controversy had increased to the point that synods were convened in many places to study the question. Church historian Eusebius (c. 260-c. 340 A.D.) describes the Asian practice:

> *All the Asian dioceses thought that in accordance with ancient tradition they ought to observe the fourteenth day of the lunar month (Nisan) as the beginning of the Paschal festival—the day on which the Jews had been commanded to sacrifice a lamb: on that day, no matter which day of the week it might be.*

And Eusebius describes the practice of western churches:

> *Nowhere else in the world was it customary to arrange their celebrations in that way: in accordance with apostolic tradition, they preserved the view which still prevails, that it was improper to end the fast on any day other than that of our Saviour's resurrection.*[5]

As a result of the synods in various places, some of the bishops widely circulated letters to Christians saying, "Never on any day other than the Lord's Day should the mystery of the Lord's resurrection from the dead be celebrated, and that on that day alone we should observe the end of the Paschal fast." This conclusion was endorsed by many bishops, including some in the Asian churches: Theophilus of Caesarea, Narcissus of Jerusalem, Victor of Rome, Palmas of Pontus, Irenaeus of the Gallic province, Bacchyllus of Corinth, the bishops in Osroene and Alexandria, and others.[6]

For the most part, the bishops of Asia did not concur. And they did not abandon their practice. Polycrates, who headed the Asian bishops, wrote to Victor and the Roman church:

We for our part keep the day scrupulously, without addition or subtraction. For in Asia great luminaries sleep who shall rise again on the day of the Lord's advent, when He is coming with glory from heaven and shall search out all His saints—such as Philip, one of the twelve apostles, who sleeps in Hierapolis with two of his daughters, who remained unmarried to the end of their days, while his other daughter lived in the Holy Spirit and rests in Ephesus. Again there is John, who leant back on the Lord's breast, and who became a sacrificing priest wearing the mitre, a martyr, and a teacher; he too sleeps in Ephesus.

Then in Smyrna there is Polycarp, bishop and martyr; and Thraseas, the bishop and martyr from Eumenia, who also sleeps in Smyrna. Need I mention Sagaris, bishop and martyr, who sleeps in Laodicea, or blessed Papirius, or Melito the eunuch, who lived entirely in the Holy Spirit, and who lies in Sardis waiting for the visitation from heaven when he shall rise from the dead?

All of these kept the fourteenth day of the month as the beginning of the Paschal festival in acccordance with the Gospel, not deviating in the least but following the rule of Faith. Last of all I too, Polycrates, the least of you all, act according to the tradition of my family, some members of which I have actually followed, for seven of them were bishops and I am the eighth, and my family have always kept the day when the people put away the leaven. So I, my friends, after spending sixty-five years in the Lord's service and conversing with Christians from all parts of the world, and going

carefully through all Holy Scripture, am not scared
of threats. Better people than I have said: 'We must
obey God rather than men.'

Polycrates added:

I could have mentioned the bishops who are with me
and whom I summoned in response to your request.
If I write their names, the list will be very long. But
though they know what an insignificant person I
am, they approve my letter, knowing that I have not
frittered away my long life but have spent it in the
service of Christ Jesus.[7]

Pope Victor's Response

Victor didn't react well to the fact that the Asian bishops
differed with the Roman church. His impulsive response was
to declare them unorthodox and to hold them up to public
ridicule and scorn. His announcement of total excommunication of all the Christians in Asia did not meet with the approval
of other bishops, however. They requested him to "turn his
mind to the things that make for peace and for unity and love
towards his neighbors."[8]

Irenaeus, on behalf of the Christians in Gaul, wrote Victor
a stern rebuke. While Irenaeus himself observed the Paschal
Feast on Sunday, he did not consider the day of observance
a matter of the major nature wherein those in disagreement
need part company. He counseled Victor that entire churches
of God could not be cut off because they observed the unbroken
tradition of their predecessors. Irenaeus said:

The dispute is not only about the day, but also about
the actual character of the fast. Some think that they
ought to fast for one day, some for two, others for
still more; some make their "day" last forty hours
on end. Such variation in the observance did not
originate in our own day, but very much earlier,

*in the time of our forefathers, who—apparently
disregarding strict accuracy—in their naive
simplicity kept up a practice which they fixed for the
time to come. In spite of that, they all lived in peace
with one another, and so do we: the divergency in
the fast emphasizes the unanimity of our faith.*

To illustrate his argument, Irenaeus cited historical incidents
where brethren differed, yet kept peace and fellowship in spite
of their different traditions of celebrating the Pasch:

*Among these were the presbyters before Soter, who
were in charge of the church of which you are the
present leader—I mean Anicetus, Pius, Hyginus,
Telesphorus, and Systus. They did not keep it [the
14th Nisan] themselves or allow those under their
wing to do so. But in spite of their not keeping it,
they lived in peace with those who came to them
from the dioceses in which it was kept, though to
keep it [in Rome] was more objectionable to those
who did not.*

*Never was this made a ground for repulsing anyone,
but the presbyters before you, even though they did
not keep it, used to send the Eucharist to Christians
from dioceses which did.*

*And when Blessed Polycarp paid a visit to Rome in
Anicetus's time, though they had minor differences
on other matters, too, they at once made peace,
having no desire to quarrel on this point. Anicetus
could not persuade Polycarp not to keep the day,
since he had always kept it with John the disciple of
our Lord and the other apostles with whom he had
been familiar; nor did Polycarp persuade Anicetus to
keep it: Anicetus said that he must stick to the
practice of the presbyters before him. Though the
position was such, they remained in communion
with each other, and in church Anicetus made way*

> *for Polycarp to celebrate the Eucharist—out of*
> *respect, obviously. They parted company in peace,*
> *and the whole Church was at peace, both those who*
> *kept the day and those who did not.*[9]

Irenaeus corresponded not only with Victor, but also with many other heads of churches concerning this controversy, presenting both sides in the interests of peace.

Some of the Palestinian bishops—Narcissus of Jerusalem, Theophilus of Caesarea, Cassius of Tyre, Clarus of Ptolemais, and others, wrote a lengthy review concerning observance of the Paschal festival. They wrote an appeal at the end of their review:

> *Try to send a copy of our letter to every diocese, so*
> *that we may not fail in our duty to those who*
> *readily deceive their own souls. We may point out to*
> *you that in Alexandria they keep the feast on the*
> *same day as we do [Sunday], for we send letters to*
> *them and they to us, to ensure that we keep the holy*
> *day in harmony and at the same time.*[10]

Council of Nicea

The Roman and other bishops who became the most powerful in the church eventually prevailed. At the Council of Nicea in 325 A.D., it was decreed that all the church must celebrate the Pasch of Christ's death and resurrection on the Sunday following 14th Nisan. The Paschal Controversy which had lasted over two centuries was settled.

The controversy had concerned only the day on which to observe The Christian Passover. It hadn't clouded Christian understanding of Passover imagery. That confusion came later, silently and subtly in the Dark Ages. It came in on the same anti-Semitic spirit which filled Constantine as he presided over the Council of Nicea. It was accompanied by Christian persecution of Jews and a growing penchant for pagan fertility symbolism.

Footnotes:

[1]Irenaeus, *Against Heresies*, iii.3.4.

[2]Melito, cited by Joseph B Tyson, *A Study of Early Christianity* (New York, The Macmillan Co., 1973), p. 249-250.

[3]Justin Martyr, *Against Apion* I,14.

[4]Epiphaneus, *Panarion Haer.* 70.10.

[5]Eusebius, *History of the Church*, Marcus Aurelius to Severus, 23.

[6]Eusebius, *op. cit.*, 23.

[7]Polycrates, quoted by Eusebius, *op. cit.*, 24.

[8]Eusebius, *op. cit.*, 24.

[9]Irenaeus, quoted by Eusebius, *op. cit.*, 24.

[10]Palestinian Bishops, quoted by Eusebius, *op. cit.*, 25.

11

NOTHING IN COMMON WITH THE JEWS

Let us have nothing in common with the detestable Jewish crowd.   *(Constantine)*

As long as Jewish Christians had influence in the church, the theology and observance of The Christian Passover was meaningful to Christians. That it was meaningful in a major way is attested to by the fact that the annual celebration of Christ's death and resurrection was named "The Christian Passover." The reference to Passover in liturgies, homilies and songs also speaks of the feast's significance to the early church.

After Gentiles came into control, Christians' understanding of and interest in Passover began to wane. Gentiles, not being grounded in the Scriptures as Jewish believers were, had little natural appreciation for Passover's meaning. Moreover, Gentiles and Jews were in tension in the church from the beginning because of their different cultural and philosophical backgrounds. Each group had unique contributions to make to the church; each had particular tendencies to err. They needed each other, but it was difficult for them to see that and deal with the differences.

Jewish persecution of Jewish Christians weakened the Jewish Christian presence in the church. Power-hungry, foolish Gentiles took advantage of the weakened Jewish position as an opportunity to forward their own personal goals for the church, elbowing out the Jews. Some Jews withdrew from the larger church into their own circles and fell into various errors. The Council of Nicea took such an anti-Semitic position that it was next to impossible for any Jew to abide it or for new Jews to come into that kind of church, so there came to be fewer and fewer Jewish Christians.

In the ensuing Dark Ages, the Gentile church, weakened spiritually by political power, turned from Scripture and fell into doctrinal error and corruption of every sort. The political power structure persecuted every protestor and also the Jews. During this time Passover's meaning was lost. Instead of Passover's typology to express the death and resurrection of the Messiah, the Gentile church adopted pagan fertility symbolism.

The Jewish Church

The church described in Acts and the Epistles was "built upon the foundation of the Prophets and Apostles, Jesus Christ Himself being the Chief Cornerstone" (Eph. 2:20). The Prophets were Jewish; the Messiah Jesus was Jewish; the Apostles were Jewish. The first believers were Jewish. Their Scriptures were the Jewish Bible. Their meeting places included the Temple and synagogues as well as private homes and public places. Their center was Jerusalem.

Between 44-68 A.D. Antioch in Syria was an important center of the Apostolic church. This was the Apostle Paul's missionary base as he took the Gospel to the Gentiles.

By 68 A.D. Peter, James, and Paul, the earliest Jewish leaders of the church, were dead. The Apostle John, based in Ephesus, provided the main leadership of the church between 68-100 A.D. He died about 95 A.D.

In the Post-Apostolic era, 100-170 A.D., the church leadership was vested in bishops who had known the Apostles and had been their disciples. Bishops Clement of Rome, Ignatius of Antioch, Polycarp of Smyrna, and Papias of Hierapolis were some of the Apostolic Fathers.

Jewish Persecution of the Jewish Church: Externally, the earliest believers headed by the Jerusalem church had the appearance of a sect of Judaism. Jewish leaders, as well as Roman authorities, considered Christianity a sect of Judaism for a number of years. The Jews gave some toleration to the newborn church until their fellowship with Gentiles was considered disloyalty to Judaism.[1]

The Jews decided they should have nothing in common with Christians. One rabbinical pronouncement said, "No man should have any dealings with the sectarians. Do not walk among them or enter their homes."[2]

Jewish leaders who did not accept Jesus as Messiah persecuted those Jews who did. The pages of the New Testament speak of this persecution.[3] While all the church came under Roman persecution, the Jewish believers bore the brunt of Jewish persecution as well. Josephus's sole mention of the Jewish church concerns persecution of Christians by the Sanhedrin following the death of Festus.[4]

Early Christians did not have the feeling that Jewish hostility and persecution was the result of simple misunderstanding which could easily be removed. As a result, they did not look for common ground in hope of compromise or friendly dialogue. Instead, they developed apologetics to meet Judaism's opposition. Jewish persecution had not made for good Christian-Jewish relations; there were bitter feelings between the two religions.

Justin Martyr, in his *Dialog with Trypho*, several times mentions the way Christ and Christians were cursed in the synagogue.[5] Justin and his successors frequently expressed the idea that always and everywhere Jews incited others against the Christians, and thus were behind much early persecution not overtly committed by them. Herod killed James, and intended to kill Peter, to please the Jews. Polycarp was murdered by a mob agitated against him by Jews.

Because of the early Jewish persecution, many Jewish believers were dispersed from Jerusalem by 66 A.D. Four years later Rome destroyed Jerusalem and dispersed all Jews from the city. Christian Jews, warned by prophecy about this desolation, had fled before the event to Pella in Perea across the Jordan where some believers had gone after the killing of James.

In 131 A.D. the Roman Emperor Hadrian declared his intention to rebuild Jerusalem as a Roman colony. It was to be a completely Gentile city named Aelia Capitolina. Hadrian also enacted a law forbidding circumcision. A Jewish leader rose up and led a rebellion in 132-135 against Rome. The famed Jewish scholar Rabbi Akiva (quoted in the *Haggadah*) considered this man the Messiah. He named him "Bar Kochba" which means "Son of the Star," an ancient title for the Messiah based on Numbers 24:17.

Christian Jews would not join with Bar Kochba's insurgents because he considered himself to be the Messiah and demanded that they denounce Jesus and follow him. They might have been willing to fight with Bar Kochba, but not under those terms. Because they did not join the Jewish rebellion, the Christian Jews were persecuted by non-Christian Jews as traitors. According to Justin Martyr, "Barcochebas, the leader of the revolt, gave orders that the Christians alone should be led to cruel punishments unless they would deny Christ and utter blasphemy."[6] Eusebius also records Bar Kochba's persecution of Christians.

Bar Kochba's followers, anticipating the Messianic kingdom, re-entered Jerusalem. They set up a temporary altar and reinstituted animal sacrifice, awaiting the soon-coming day when the Temple would be rebuilt and Messiah Bar Kochba would reign. The Passover lamb sacrifice would soon be resumed.

Hadrian crushed the Jewish revolt in 135. The Jews who had entered Jerusalem were again driven from the city. After 135, all Jews (Christian Jews included) were forbidden to enter Jerusalem. The city was renamed Aelia. The church there came under the leadership of Gentile bishops. The Jewish believers scattered by this Roman war took refuge in the mountains of Galilee along with non-Christian Jews, while Gentile believers had been settling mainly with other Gentiles in the coastal towns of Palestine. Isolation from each other helped to aggravate differences between Jewish and Gentile Christians. The Gentiles, unchecked by the Jews, fell into the errors to which they were more prone. The Jews, unchecked by Gentiles, fell into the errors to which they were more prone.

Jewish Tendencies to Error: Palestine Christians from the earliest days were divided into two distinct branches—the Jewish and the Gentile—due to cultural and religious background diversity. Each group had its distinctive contributions to make to the church; each had its tendencies to certain errors.

When the Jews erred, they tended to err in the direction of exclusiveness or of feeling superior to Gentile believers. They also erred in the direction of looking to the Law as a means of salvation. (Both of these tendencies had also been a problem under the Old Covenant. God had to command love for the stranger. His people tended to not understand the Spirit of the Law and the meaning of sacrifice.) The Jews continued in firm adherence to the Scriptures which God had given them, but had a problem of properly reconciling New Covenant with Old.

Distinctly-Jewish sects arose in the early church. Some, such as the Ebionites and Jewish Gnostics, went far astray from truth. Some of these groups produced their own Gospels, unaccepted by the church as a whole.

The Matter of "Judaizing": One of the greatest struggles of the early predominately-Jewish church was discerning how Christ fulfilled the Law without destroying it. How were they to respond to the Law in the light of the Gospel? For example, in the matter of Passover, what were they to do with God's command to observe Passover "forever—in all their generations?'' Historical records indicate that many in the early church continued to celebrate the Exodus Passover, but with emphasis on its fulfillment at Calvary. They eliminated the sacrifice of the lamb because Christ had fulfilled animal sacrifice.

In Laodicea, about 170 A.D., a problem arose about observance of Passover. Possibly some were erroneously saying lambs should be sacrificed and eaten as part of the observance. (But probably that historical view of the Laodicean problem is incorrect since any Jew who would be inclined toward the Law regarding sacrificing the lambs surely realized the lambs could not be sacrificed in Laodicea according to the Law.) Whatever the specific problem, Melito, Bishop of Sardis, and Apollinarius, Bishop of Hierapolis, (both "Protopaschites," or "Quartodecimans"—Jews who celebrated The Christian Passover on 14th Nisan) dealth with it. They said those who had caused the problem were trying to take the church back to the Law.[7]

Leaders in opposition to Jewish legalists were other Jews— the Jewish Apostles and their disciples. Paul dealt with the Jewish Ebionites (who denied the divinity of Jesus and opposed Paul's teachings), with the Jewish Gnostics (who phantomized Jesus and denied His humanity), and with Jewish Legalizers (who taught that circumcision and keeping the Law were necessary for salvation). Paul, the Jew, dealt with these problems of Jewish error. He also dealt with errors of Gentile philosophy. The Apostle John, who became the chief leader of the church after Peter, James and Paul died, also dealt with error. For example, he writes in the Revelation of the Nicolaitans, a Gnostic Jewish sect.

The word "Judaizing" does not appear in the Bible. It is a term developed by prejudiced people implying that the error of some Christian Jews was a characteristic of all Christian Jews. Historians trace part of the charges of "Judaizing" to ignorance, to church politicking, and to rising anti-Semitism in the church.

The Quartodecimans, including the Apostles John and Philip, were originally a respected and significant force in the church. There were many Christians who disagreed with them. However, those differing respected each other. But the Quartodecimans fell victim to opportunist and anti-Semitic individuals who used the fear of legalism, seen in Ignatius and others, to make plausible—at least to those who wanted to believe it—the charges of "Judaizing **heresy**" leveled against them. A close look at some specific Judaizing charges reveals them to be actually the rationalizing of western prejudice against the Asian church.

Hippolytus attacked the Quartodecimans with the charge that they "pay heed to that which is written in the Law" (as though the writings of Moses had been thrown out of the Bible when the writings of the Apostles were brought in). He accused the Quartodecimans of being "lovers of strife" when he himself engendered strife with the charged words, "they [Quartodecimans] pay no attention to the fact that it [the Law] was enacted for the **Jews, who were to kill the true Passover**."[8]

Hippolytus was familiar with Polycrates' correspondence with Victor about the Christian Passover. He knew how the Quartodeciman leaders had dealt with the Laodician problem by not allowing legalism. But he chose to ignore that. Some historians conclude that Hippolytus and others (such as the writer of Pseudo-Tertullian) were either ignorant or uncharitable.

Valid and invalid charges of legalizing ("Judaizing") have always been a part of church history. Those dealing with the subject of the Christian Passover must deal with that issue.

"Judaizing" charges grew to extremes. By John Calvin's time (1509-1564) anything in the Easter service which resembled the early Christian Passover was open to be called "Judaic" (something bad). Calvin was accused of "Judaizing Christianity" because he used unleavened bread in the Easter service.

Rise of the Gentile Church

The Jewish church suffered the early Jewish persecution. Jews also suffered under Nero's persecution in 64 A.D. The Jewish believers experienced the Jewish persecution of the Bar Kochba rebellion. They were also victims in the later Roman persecutions. Besides suffering more persecution than the Gentile believers, they experienced the prejudice of Gentile Christians which allowed power-hungry, politicking Gentiles to take advantage of their dispersion and weakened condition. All this paved the way for a Gentile church to rise to leadership.

The Gentile church which rose to leadership was the Roman Church. As early as 93-97 A.D., Clement, Bishop of Rome, had asserted dominance in his dealings with the Corinthians. Rome was the only church in the west which had had dealing with the Apostles. Irenaeus of Lyons in 185 spoke of the Roman church as founded by Peter and Paul. The Roman bishop was regarded as first among bishops because Rome was the Empire's capital. The Roman church was largely Gentile following a decree of Claudius in 49 A.D. banishing Jews from Rome.

As the Gentiles gained power, they made significant contributions to the Body of Christ. The Gentiles, who were pagan converts for the most part, could more readily and gladly grasp the concepts of the universal church and the law of liberty in the Gospel. As they related to Gentile philosophies, great apologists and preachers arose from the Gentile ranks. Gentiles carried the Gospel to their contacts throughout the world. Jews alone could not have formed the solid foundation of the church that would take the Gospel to the entire world. Gentiles were needed to help Jewish believers break out of human traditions and look objectively at God's New Covenant and plan for the world. They could help Jews get free from their tendency to fall into legalism.

Gentile Tendencies to Error: Gentile church leaders dealt decisively with what they saw as Jewish errors. However, with

the Jewish church diminished there was no longer a balance
of power so that Jews could check Gentiles in **their** errors.

When Gentiles erred, they tended to err in the direction of
feeling smugly that they had been given the New Covenant
instead of the Jews rather than **with** them. Justin Martyr might
have erred in this direction. Gentiles tended to think Jesus came
to destroy the Law, not fulfill it (the reverse of what Jesus
taught).

Gentile Christians usually came from a background devoid
of Scripture knowledge. They did not have a natural appreciation for, allegiance to, or comprehension of the Scriptures. It
was not difficult for them to disregard the Scriptures, especially
the Law and Prophets which they misunderstood, overlooked,
or actually discarded in the early church struggle to break free
from the erroneous legalizers. They found it easy to disregard
Passover and other major institutions of the Mosaic Covenant
and not try to do anything with the teachings there. One
historian (with the summarizing ability that hindsight provides)
commented, "The opposite extreme [of legalism] is a false
Christianity which may be called the Paganizing or Gnostic
heresy. This exaggerates the Pauline view of the distinction
of Christianity from Judaism and sunders Christianity from its
historical basis."[9]

Gentiles tended not to revere even the Apostolic writings.
It cannot be stated that continued Jewish leadership would have
kept the church in Scripture, but the fact is that the Gentile
church did not stay centered in Scripture. Rather, it exalted
traditions and the word of men that contradicted God's revelation in the writings canonized as Scripture. Without the Word
of God as a daily guide, the Gentile church succumbed to the
doctrinal error, superstition and moral decadence of the Dark
Ages.

Gentiles were drawn away from Scripture not only because
they lacked background in it, but because of the appeal of Greek
and Roman philosophy and mystery religions. They were

influenced by Gnosticism, Manicheanism, Neoplatonism, and many other heresies and errors.

The Marcion Heresy: Getting away from the revealed Word of God opened the way for Gentiles to fall into a deadly error— the belief that they alone had become inheritors of the New Covenant (not with Jews, but instead of them). The church was easy prey for the Marcion heresy.

Marcion, the son of a bishop, came to Rome in 140 A.D. and for several years saturated the city with his teaching that there were two gods. One god, the god of the Old Testament and of the Jews, was evil and the author of all evil. The other God, who had been unknown until revealed in Jesus, was the good God of love who delivered men from the evil god of the Jews. Marcion hated the Jews and the Old Testament. He completely rejected the Jewish tradition and rejected many of the Apostolic writings as well. He established his own canon of acceptable writings. He venerated the Apostle Paul to such a degree that Paul's name and epistles became associated with Marcionism. He pitted Paul against the Jews. Perhaps this led to the incorrect charges that Paul was against the Old Testament and his own people, the Jews.

Eventually the church condemned Marcion's teachings, but not before Marcion heresy had gained a strong foothold and spread throughout the world. Marcion churches were established in many places, and Marcionism lasted into the fifth century.

Constantine and Christianity

In addition to persecution by Jews, the church experienced waves of persecution under the Roman Emperors Nero (in 64 A.D.), Trajan (98-117), Hadrian (117-138), Antonius Pius (138-161), Marcus Aurelius (161-180), Decius (249-251), Valerian (253-260), and Diocletian (303-311). The most violent and extensive persecution came under Diocletian.

Diocletian's persecution was his attempt to strengthen the

Empire by wiping out Christianity. Christians were not loyal to Rome in that they refused to be included with others in the monotheistic state religion. His persecution did not work. As Tertullian put it, the martyrs' blood was the seed of the faith. Also, the populace was getting sick of the bloodshed and were sympathizing with the Christians. Grudgingly, one of Diocletian's appointed co-emperors, Galerius, signed an edict on his deathbed granting toleration to the Christians.

Constantine, the next emperor, saw that Diocletian had failed to crush the church with the greatest of all persecutions and he realized that more persecution was not likely to succeed. He tried a new approach—making use of the church as an ally to save the classical culture of Rome from the threat of the wandering barbarian tribes. People of Constantine's day were ready for a single world religion. Christians, strong in Egypt and Syria, had to be reconciled at any cost. But Christians refused to worship any god but their own. If the Empire was to have their full friendship, it must become a Christian state.

Constantine suddenly "became a Christian" in 312 A.D. The word passed around that he had experienced a divine miracle and seen a bright cross in the sky and heard the words, "By this sign conquer."

An additional word (or a contradicting one) was that he had dreamed he was to put Christian symbols upon his soldiers. Astute historians wonder if such visions actually occurred and Constantine genuinely became a Christian, or if his favoring the church was a matter of political expediency. His behavior was not according to Scripture's guidelines for Christians. He kept the position of *Pontifex Maximus*, chief priest of the pagan state religion, a cult of the sun. In 321, he issued a royal decree that named the first day of the week (the day Christians had been calling "the Lord's Day") "Sun's Day." He murdered his own young son and wife in 326 for political or personal reasons. He killed others who might have had claim to his throne. He was not baptized until he was on his deathbed in 337 A.D.

Constantine, with Licinius his co-emperor between 311 and 324, guaranteed Christians freedom from persecution and gave Christian clergy favored positions of political power and privilcgc. Overnight, Christianity's lot suddenly changed from being severely persecuted to being pampered. A flood of "new converts" joined the church, many of them more superficial than those earlier Christians whose commitment had been strong enough to withstand persecution.

Although Constantine had reconciled Christianity to the Roman State, he saw that all Christians were not reconciled to each other. Two major church controversies were raging— the Arian and the Paschal controversies. A divided church could not help unify the Empire. In 325 A.D., shortly after he had become sole Emperor by putting Licinius to death, Constantine called the Council of Nicea for the purpose of unifying the church and thereby strengthening his empire. Later that year Christianity officially became the state religion.

The Council of Nicea

At the Council of Caesarea (196 A.D.) churchmen had voted to hold the annual Christian Passover on the Sunday following the 14th Nisan, rather than on the 14th. This Council had included only Gentile bishops. Either the Jewish bishops were not invited or they declined to come. The Passover decree of this council was not accepted or followed by those who disagreed with it. So the world-wide church controversy about the day of observance continued.

At another earlier council (Arles, 314 A.D.) called by Constantine before he was sole Emperor, it had also been decreed that the Christian Passover should be celebrated on one and the same day everywhere and that the Bishop of Rome should fix that day. The decree of this council also went unheeded.

Churches in Syria and Mesopotamia continued to follow "the custom of the Jews" and celebrated on the 14th, while the western churches (Italy, Africa, Spain, Britain, etc.) observed Sunday.

Meanwhile, in 319 A.D., a major new church controversy had begun over the views of one Arius regarding the divinity of Christ and the nature of the Trinity. Arius's doctrine regarding the person of Christ was largely taken from Ebionite doctrine. (Ebionites were Jews who called themselves Christians but denied the divinity of Jesus and opposed the writings of Paul.)

Shortly after he became sole Emperor in 324, Constantine planned the Council of Nicea which convened in 325 A.D. Churchmen from the world over were invited. Approximately 300 bishops and numerous priests and deacons came.

Jews Not Invited: Each of the two main topics to be dealt with—the Arian controversy and the Paschal controversy—involved a minority Jewish-influenced viewpoint versus a majority basically-Gentile viewpoint. Constantine apparently began his plan to unify the church by simply not inviting any Jewish representatives to the Council. (It is possible Jewish church leaders were invited and refused to come, but other facts about the Council lead to the former conclusion.) The lists of those present at the Council shows them all to have had Greek names. None of those present had characteristic Jewish names. The Palestinian delegates were from the coastal cities where mainly Gentiles lived. It is known that there were Jewish bishops in Palestine at the time.[10]

Constantine's Control: Constantine assumed the position of moderator at the Council. He opened the Council by not reading, but burning, the lists of complaints against each other which the bishops had presented to him. Then he gave a speech on unity.

Constantine took a militant anti-Semitic position at the

Council. This may have reflected his true personal feelings, or it may have simply been the stance he considered most expedient. Regarding the Christian Passover, Constantine said:

> We would have nothing in common with that most hostile people, the Jews, for we have received from the Redeemer another way of honoring God, and harmoniously adopting this method, we would withdraw ourselves from the evil fellowship of the Jews. For what they pompously assert is really utterly absurd: that we cannot keep this feast at all without their instruction. . . . It is our duty to have nothing in common with the murderers of our Lord.[11]

The fact that Christianity had never had religious fellowship with non-Christian Jews means the Jews referred to were Christian Jews. The reference to Jews instructing Christians how to observe the Christian Passover feast could only be applicable to Christian Jews, as non-Christian Jews did not tell Christians how to observe Passover. The fellowship from which Constantine wanted the church to withdraw was fellowship with Christian Jews.

Fear and Prejudice: Constantine's anti-Semitic stance was actively endorsed by some Council delegates and unopposed by others. In reference to the Arian issue, it has been noted that "many of the members of the council might have been deterred from expressing their real belief, as some few of them undoubtedly were, from the fear of exile or deposition."[12] Undoubtedly the same holds true regarding the Passover issue. It had been only a little over a decade since Diocletian's persecution; some of the delegates bore scars from torture under that emperor. This emperor could also turn to persecution if he wanted to. Certainly most had some realization of Constantine's ulterior motives, but for the worldwide good of the church they had to try to discern how best to walk on the eggshells. Undoubtedly some in attendance were the new political breed seeking to control the church. Those were not there for spiritual reasons. There was demonstrably an impatience with what was, justly or unjustly, perceived as Jewish influence in the errors which the Council sought to correct. Athanasius, a delegate to the Council, said of the Arians, "All their stupid doctrine was Jewish." Bishops Alexander of Alexandria and Lucifer of Cagliari agreed.[13]

For whatever reason, the Gentile bishops betrayed the Jewish Christians at the Council. And they departed from the Lord in not loving the non-Christian Jews. Either they actually sided with Constantine, or they let his anti-Semitism go unopposed.

Results of the Council: The Paschal Controversy was "settled" at the Council of Nicea—not theologically, but politically. It was settled by eliminating one of the viewpoints.

Church law had been laid down. No longer could any Christian celebrate Christian Passover the way John, Philip and other Jews had celebrated it. All were required to celebrate on the Sunday following the 14th. Once-respected "Quartodecimans" who persisted in the belief handed down to them from the Apostles, would henceforth be called heretics. Their way of celebrating on 14th Nisan, which had once been accepted was now forbidden.

Churches in Mesopotamia protested the Council's decision saying that "this was the first time that the ancient tradition, through complaisance for Constantine, had been departed from."[14]

It is inconceivable that Jewish Christians could have escaped a struggle with bitterness after the Council of Nicea. It is understandable that they withdrew into themselves. It is understandable that non-Christian Jews would have no interest in investigating the beliefs of such a church.

The Council set the precedent for future councils. The breach between Gentile and Jewish Christians continually grew wider. Some of the isolated Jewish Christian groups managed to survive a few hundred years, but most Christian Jews were absorbed into Gentile culture or fell away from sound doctrine. By the 5th century, Christian Jews were scarce.

As far as Christian Passover is concerned, the beginning of the Dark Ages can be set at 325 A.D. with the Council of Nicea. Along with turning their backs on Jews, the Gentiles turned their backs on the Jewish Scriptures. They disallowed Jewish input to their faith, lifestyle, and worship. They became persecutors of the Jews. In place of the Exodus Passover story to inspire a sense of justice and freedom for all men, the Gentile church had the words and example of power-hungry leaders who taught oppression. It took a major reformation centuries later to begin to undo the horror and destruction the church brought on the world when the Gentiles at Nicea formally adopted the policy of having "nothing in common with the Jews."

Anti-Semitic Evidences: The rule of Sunday instead of the 14th was not the only Passover rule the political-religious leaders made. They further decreed that whenever the 14th Nisan fell on a Sunday, Christians were to celebrate the Christian Passover on the next Sunday following. This rule was made not out of theological concern to observe Sunday as the proper day, but out of the stated concern to put distance between Gentiles and Jews.

Later adoption of the solar calendar put even more distance between the 14th Nisan and the Christian's new date for the annual observance.

Eliminating the Jewish viewpoint was rationalized as a necessity to protect the church from being "Judaized." But the true historical context of the Council's attitudes and decrees is further illustrated by the earlier church legislation (305 A.D.) of bishops in Elvira, Spain which forbade trade, intermarriage or social contact between Christian and Jew.

Religious-Political Laws Against Judaism

The Roman political-religious structure did not limit its prejudice and control by law and force to those within the Christian church; it legislated against Judaism as well. Following the Council of Nicea, Jews in Palestine were forbidden to make converts. Jerusalem (by then filled with churches) was forbidden to Jews. Jews of Palestine were barred from public office and forbidden to build new synagogues.

The Jews were not simply passive about the legislation against them; they expressed their contempt in various ways. One way in which Jews scorned Christians was by nailing wicked Haman to a cross (instead of hanging him on a gallows) during Purim festivities. The obvious allusion to Christ's crucifixion angered Christians and provoked riots.[15] In an extreme case in 415 A.D., Jews in Antioch put a Christian child on a cross and scourged him to death.[16]

Emperor Justinian (482-565) barred Judaism's celebration of Passover until after the Christian celebration. He also made it a law that synagogues use Greek versions of Scripture and that Christian priests interpret them.

In Spain (589 A.D.) Jews were forbidden to raise their own children (who were baptized by force). During the 600s, all Jews caught practicing Judaism were enslaved, their land confiscated, and their children taken to convents to be brought up by the church.

In 614 A.D., Jews again had some power against Christians. Under Benjamin of Tiberius, they combined forces with Persia to kill 90,000 Christians in Jerusalem in an attempt to rid Palestine of its Christian rulers.

Again the balance of power reversed. In 630 A.D., Byzantine Emperor Heraclius conquered the neo-Persian empire. With Palestine again in Christian hands, the monks and priests

demanded extermination of the Jews. The only Jews to survive were those who escaped to Babylon, Egypt, and Arabia.

Growing Persecution of Jews

Jews and Christians had both demonstrated that "power
corrupts." When given political power, each had persecuted
the other in the first seven centuries since the birth of Christianity. From the Middle Ages onward the church had more
political power than Judaism. Religious history through the
Dark Ages includes the hideous record of Christian persecution of the Jews. Much of the persecution had to do directly
with Passover.

Political and religious persecution of Jews next led to expul-
sion of the Jews from many countries of the world. Jews were
expelled in the 11th century from many German towns, and
their land seized. In 1290 they were ordered to leave England;
in 1306 France; in 1421 Austria and later Bavaria; in 1492
Spain. Torture and murder of Jews increased. The Crusades
which began in 1096 and lasted two centuries, and the Spanish
and Portugese Inquisitions of the 15th and 16th centuries
slaughtered thousands upon thousands of Jews in the name
of Christ. The tormentors wore crosses. The Nazis, too, carried out the Holocaust under a form of a cross, the swastika.

The Fourth Lateran Council, convened by Rome in 1215
A.D., decreed that all Jews had to wear a distinguishing patch
on their clothing. Jews were said to have been born of demonic
beings. They were blamed for calamities such as the Bubonic
Plague.

Religious leaders sometimes tried to stop mob action against
Jews, but often incited it. Martin Luther (1483-1546) who at
first urged people to "deal kindly with the Jews," in later years
wrote a series of anti-Semitic pamphlets. He advised his
followers to burn down Jewish homes and synagogues, to
destroy Jewish religious literature, and to kill rabbis who would

not be silent. "Let us drive them out of the country for all time," he wrote. He said, "To sum up, dear princes and nobles who have Jews in your domains, if this advice of mine does not suit you, then find a better one so that you and we may all be free of this insufferable devilish burden—the Jews."[17]

The Charge of Decide

Thomas Aquinas (1226-1274), echoing Hippolytus, Chryso-stom, and other earlier church leaders, had said Jews were condemned to perpetual servitude for the act of deicide. On Good Friday, not far from Passover on the calendar, Chris-tians were sometimes stirred to emotional frenzy about "the Jews crucifying Jesus." This incited mobs to attack Jews. The charge of deicide has rung through the ages. Even today many Jews have been derisively called "Christ killers."

This attitude is totally alien from the theology and attitude of the early church, as reflected in the New Testament writings. The Apostles did indeed charge Jewish religious leaders of the day with responsibility for Jesus' death (Acts 4:10-11). And they charged the Jewish nation of that day (who had been gathered in the one place, Jerusalem, for Passover) with responsibility (Acts 2:22-23; 3:12-17). But they also charged the **Gentile** leaders and the **Gentile** common people of that day: "Against thy holy child Jesus, whom thou hast anointed, both Herod [half-Jewish leader], and Pontius Pilate [Roman leader], with the Gentiles, and the people of Israel, were gathered together" (Acts 4:27). The Jewish leaders, the Roman leaders, the Jewish people, the Gentile people—**all** were indicted.

But the sin of Jesus' generation in crucifying Him did not pass on to succeeding generations just because the crowd which cried "crucify him!" also said, "His blood be upon us and our children" (Matt. 27:25). Regardless of what people say, God's law says that children are not guilty because of their parents' iniquity (Jer. 31:29-30). They may not be free from the consequences of their parents' sins, but they are free from the guilt.

And as to the sin of that generation who crucified Jesus, Jesus forgave them from the cross, saying, "Father, forgive them, for they know not what they do" (Lk. 23:34).

As to the term, "deicide," there is no such thing. No one can kill God. The early church believed no one could kill God's anointed, the Messiah. There are statements of theology in the writings of the early church leaders which demonstrate that they would never have called anyone a "Christ killer." The New Testament writers declare that no one **could** be a Christ killer; no man had power over Jesus to kill Him. "It must be that offenses come, and woe to him by whom they come," (Matt. 18:7 and Lk. 17:1), but if it had not been God's Passover plan, Jesus could not have been crucified. Jesus was crucified "by the determinate counsel and foreknowledge of God" (Acts 2:23). God carried this out by "using" men who chose to sin. Those Jewish leaders, Roman leaders, Jewish people and Gentile people who Peter said were gathered together against the Lord and His Anointed One (Acts 4:25-27) "were gathered together for to do whatsoever Thy [God's] hand and Thy counsel determined before to be done" (Acts 4:27-28). People did have a choice in the matter, and they chose wrong. And God used this. Just as He had used Pharaoh, who continually made the wrong choice, to accomplish His purposes in Egypt, God used the hard-hearted sinners of Jesus' generation to accomplish His purpose of providing the Passover Lamb. The Father had sent the Son, the Lamb of God, to die for the sin of the world. (John 1:29) Jesus was "the Lamb slain from the foundation of the world" in divine planning. (Rev. 13:8) The Father gave His Lamb for the world. (John 3:16) Jesus, the Passover, **had** to die in God's plan. (I Cor. 5:7; Is. 53:4-7; Rom. 3:23-25) Just before His crucifixion, Jesus said no one could take His life from Him because He had power over life and death. But He could, and would, lay down His life willingly, and then take it back again from death. (John 10:15-18)

The Blood Libel

In the Dark Ages, Christians were ignorant not only of Biblical Christian Passover theology, but also of Judaism's Passover beliefs and practices. This became part of the basis for still another type of persecution of Jews at Passover time. Gentiles accused the Jews of sacrificing humans to obtain blood for their Passover ceremony. This "blood libel" was leveled at Jews for centuries.

In 1475 an entire Jewish community was exterminated in Trent, Italy because of a malicious false rumor that they had killed an infant to obtain blood for Passover.

Corrupt clergy in the 1500's inflamed crowds with the ritual murder charges, quite possibly to draw attention away from the church decadence which shortly thereafter finally called forth the full force of the Reformation.

The blood libel lasted from the 12th through the 16th centuries, and was resurrected in the 18th and 19th centuries, with some incidents in the 20th century. It was part of Nazi Germany's proaganda against the Jews.

Many riots and pogroms occurred at Passover time. There was a riot in York, England on Passover 1189 in which many Jews died. Pogroms and massacres occurred from 1881 to 1905 in Russia at the Passover-Easter season.

From Christian Passover to Easter

Developing hand in hand with isolation from the Jews and persecution of them, was the exaltation of traditions over Scripture. This led to the doctrinal errors which the Reformation had to address. It also led to the common acceptance of pagan fertility customs which corrupted Christian Passover worship.

(The Reformation leaders did not get around to renewing the church in this specific area. The problem survived into the 20th century.)

The Pasch was renamed "Easter." The symbolism and customs of the feast changed. Only a few traditions survived as reminders of its former nature: sunrise services and the "Easter Candle" (reminiscent of the days when Christian Passover was an evening-to-dawn observance); wearing new clothes at Easter (from the Christian Passover practice of giving the newly-baptized believers new white linen robes as a symbol of new life); lambs molded of butter, cake, or candy (symbols of the Paschal Lamb).

For the most part, the Gentile church turned from Biblical redemption imagery to fertility symbolism in its celebration of Christ's death and resurrection. Magic and superstition touched even the nobler traditions that had survived. Molded lambs given by priests to parishoners in Finland were supposed to have magical protective powers. Fire from the church Paschal Candle was carried away by lit tapers with superstitious and occult intentions. It was thought it protected from lightening. Boys in Germany ran through fields with bundles of straw set with fire from the Paschal candle to insure good crops the following year. Young people gazed into mirrors by light from the Paschal candle to tell their fortunes for the coming year.

Eostre, Goddess of Spring

The English word "Easter" and the German *Ostern* come from a common origin (*Eostre, Eastur, Ostara, Ostar*) which to Norsemen meant the season of the rising (growing) sun. The sun rises in the east (*ost*), giving new life to crops. Bede, the eighth century theologian and historian who introduced the word Easter to the church, said it referred to an Anglo-Saxon goddess of dawn and spring known as *Eostre* or *Ostara*, whose principal festival was kept at the vernal equinox.

It is probable that Eostre/Ostara is the Anglo-Saxon version of Ishtar, the Summerian goddess of love and war who in Canaan evolved into a moon goddess and wife of Baal. According to Summerian lore, Ishtar was the wife of the Summerian god, Tammuz. Both are spoken of in the Bible—Tammuz in Ezekiel 8:14 and Ishtar, called Ashtoreth and Queen of Heaven, in Judges 2:13, Judges 10:6, Jeremiah 44:17f, and elsewhere.

When Tammuz died, Ishtar followed him to the underworld, leaving the earth deprived of its fertility. She and Tammuz were rescued from death when the Queen of the Dead allowed a heavenly messenger to sprinkle them with the water of life. This allowed them to return to the light of the sun for six months of each year. For the other six they had to return to the land of death.

Worship of Ishtar as a nature goddess had spread throughout the ancient world. In Phoenicia and Syria her name had become Astarte. Her husband earlier called Baal, and known as Tammuz farther east, became Adon or Adonai in Phoenicia and Syria. In Greece, Ishtar and Tammuz became Aphrodite and Adonis; in Asia Minor they became Cybele and Attis. Diana of the Ephesians (Acts 19:27) probably traces to Ishtar.

Easter Bunny and Easter Eggs

Gone with Passover symbolism was the Passover lamb. In its place was the Easter hare. The Easter hare was once a bird which the goddess Eostre changed into a four-footed creature. The Egyptian hare was a fertility symbol. The hare, a most fertile animal, symbolized the abundant new life of spring. He was the emblem of Aphrodite (Eostre) in Greece.

The eggs which the Easter Bunny produces and gives to children are themselves fertility symbols. The origin of the Easter egg is traced to Indo-European fertility lore. In ancient Egypt, Phoenicia, and India the universe is said to have been born from a mighty world egg. The ancient peoples of Egypt, Persia, Greece, Rome, and China exchanged eggs at their spring fertility festivals. In Babylonia, eggs were presented to the goddess of fertility, Astarte (Eostre).

Christians took the egg and put upon it their own symbolism. Augustine saw in the egg a symbol of the hope of eternal life: an egg is that which has not yet come to fruition. Others saw the resurrection in the egg: it symbolized the rock tomb from which Christ emerged in new life.

Eggs were once forbidden food during Lent, so they were blessed, decorated and given as Easter gifts celebrating the day they could again be eaten. Record of Easter egg use in Western Europe begins in the 15th century. In parts of Eastern Europe and the Balkan countries, eggs were elaborately painted with symbols, often Roman crosses and swastikas.

Other Legends, Customs and Superstitions

Uncountable legends grew up about birds, flowers, animals, trees and just about everything in life, relating to Easter. Just one example is the legend of the robin. Its breast is said to have become red when blood from Christ's wounds stained the breast of a robin which flew to the cross to pluck a thorn from His head.

Origins of Mardi Gras are traced to medieval customs pertaining to the beginning of Lent.

Ham came to be a popular Easter food because the pig was widely regarded as a symbol of good luck and prosperity. (Piggy banks still carry through the ancient association of the pig with prosperity.)

Christians, "free from the law of unleavened breads," developed their own customs involving leavened breads. Pretzels originated as a Lenten bread made without the Lenten-forbidden foods of fat, eggs, and milk. They were called "little arms" (*bracellae* in Latin; *brezel* or *prezel* in German) because they were shaped like two arms folded in prayer as a reminder that Lent was a time of penance and devotion. Hot cross buns became popular after their origin in 1361 as a Good Friday feature in St. Alban's Abbey. These were similar to the cakes associated with worship of Diana—wheaten cakes made at spring festivals and marked with a cross. Many superstitions grew up concerning hot cross buns. People kept them through the year, eating them as medicine or wearing them as charms against disease, lightening and shipwreck. People believed their homes would be protected from fire if they ate hot cross buns on Good Friday.

A popular bonfire custom of pagan origin was admitted to the Roman Church liturgy as an Easter custom after the church first rejected, then tolerated, then finally adopted it. Many fire customs had to do with driving away the demons of winter. Sometimes hideous effigies of these winter demons were made. There were then beaten, burned or "drowned."

Many Easter fertility traditions developed in the middle ages. One Easter custom—gently striking a girl with a fertility branch, "the rod of life" —evolved into the custom of throwing the bridal bouquet. Water taken from springs at Easter was kept in bottles throughout the year to be sprinkled on brides and bridegrooms before they went to the church to be married. Some customs had clear origins in the occult. Fertility customs involved various kinds of sprinkling with water, heaving boys and girls in chairs, and other practices now seen only on the pages of history books.

Reformation

While many in the middle ages were overcome by spiritual darkness, others were not. There were always those who had the light of God's Word. With time and the right circumstances they were able to organize, and reformation touched the church and the world.

It was the Word of God which provided the light in the darkness. To the degree Christians returned to the Bible, they returned to the love of God, sound doctrine, moral purity, and social justice. The Scriptures gave light about the Jews, speaking of God's eternal covenant with them and His promises for their future in His Kingdom. There was no "Easter fertility cult" in God's plan for the world.

One of the important forerunners of the Protestant Reformation was John Wycliffe (c1328-1384) whose followers were called Lollards. In 1382 Wycliffe provided a translation of the New Testament in the English language. There followed in 1384 an English translation of the Old Testament. The Bible guided the Lollards who influenced later reformation efforts, but the Bible could not be made available to people in a wide-spread way until after the invention in 1454 of moveable type. In 1525 the English-speaking world received the Tyndale Bible.

John Calvin (1509-1564) was one of the Reformers who took the Word of God to heart. He had an appreciation for the Old Testament as well as the New. Calvin, and those most influenced by him (Reformed, Puritan, Presbyterian, Separatist, and other groups), were not hostile to Jews.

Calvin considered the annual church feast of Easter so paganized that at one point he did not observe it. However, he did not reinstitute the early church "Christian Passover" in its place. Although he studied and wrote dissertations on many subjects, Calvin did not recover for the church a full understanding of how Passover relates to redemption in Jesus.

Calvin's followers in Holland made that country a safe haven for persecuted Jews and Protestants. Jews found refuge in Holland in the 1500s. Some persecuted Calvinists—the Puritans—found refuge there in the following century. Jews and Puritans rubbed shoulders in Holland.

Puritans had great influence in England from about 1560 to 1660. They, like Calvin, had taken to heart the entire Bible.

Familiarity with the Law and Prophets, as well as the Apostles' writings, gave them the knowledge that Jewish and Gentile believers shared the same destiny in the Lord. The Puritans contributed significantly to the end of Christian hostility toward Jews. It was Puritans who in 1649 successfully petitioned the government to repeal England's 1290 edict banishing Jews from that country. They also petitioned England at that time to work toward establishing a homeland for the Jews in Palestine. Puritans, and later Evangelicals descended from them, worked unceasingly in England for the state of Israel, playing a major role in bringing about the Balfour Declaration of 1917. The Evangelicals also began mission outreach to call Jews into fellowship with Messiah Jesus and with themselves (an endeavor which Jews did not appreciate).

Puritans frowned upon the paganzied church feasts. In Puritan England Parliament struck Christmas, Easter and Whitsuntide (Pentecost) from the calendar.

The New World

In 1492 Jews were expelled from Spain. That same year, perhaps not by coincidence, Christopher Columbus (thought by some to have been a Marrano—a "Christian" outwardly to escape persecution, but a secret Jew inwardly), discovered the new world. Jews as well as persecuted Christians arrived early in the New World to make it their home. Jews were involved with Christians in giving American society its new base, shaping the country into a nation offering freedom of religion. They fought with Christians in the Revolutionary War.

Baptists, who were a people steeped in the Bible, played a major role shaping America's policy of religious freedom. Roger Williams (1603-1683), father of the Baptist movement in America, wrote a tract in 1644 on separation of church and state. In this he proclaimed that Gentile and Jew alike must have freedom of religion.

Puritans, more than any others, gave America its foundation in the principles of Scripture. The Puritans knew in depth the Law and the Prophets which contain the Bible's great foundational teachings on justice. They saturated the country with God's Word and helped make America a nation that "proclaimed liberty throughout the land," living out the political liberty and justice for all inspired by the Exodus story.

In America, as well as in England, the Puritans did not celebrate the annual church feasts which they considered paganized. They knew the Exodus story as well as the New Testament. Since they were refugees from oppression, it was the social implications of the Exodus story which spoke most to them. They quoted from the Exodus often, applying elements of the Biblical account to their own political situation. They felt they were like the Israelites delivered by God's hand. The meaning of Passover was for the Puritans, as it was for the Jews, related to temporal sufferings and deliverance. Puritan theology did not included any annual "Passover" observance for them, however. Passover's meaning for them found expression in their daily social and political activism, not in any religious ritual. They knew Jews: they knew of the Jewish Seder. But they did not consider that annual ritual theirs to observe. They rejected the paganized Easter. Either they did not know of the early church "Christian Passover," or they rejected that kind of annual commemoration as well.

With Puritan influence so strong, hardly anyone in America's early days celebrated Easter. Exceptions were in Louisiana and Maryland settled by Catholics.

Later immigrants brought their Easter customs with them, and these began to take hold in America as they had in Europe. Mardi Gras before Lent became big in certain cities. The Easter Parade, Easter bonnets, chocolate eggs, Easter baskets, and a cuter-than-ever Easter bunny have developed as American Easter traditions. American churches with strong Biblical emphasis do not relate these customs to any church belief. Churches instead have developed customs such as union Good Friday services and Resurrection Sunday sunrise services. But Christian individuals still participate in Easter customs, and the church still calls its annual commemoration of Christ's death and resurrection "Easter."

Footnotes:

[1] See Acts 24:14-15; 28:22; 12:1f; 21:27f.

[2] Chaim Potok, *Wanderings: Chaim Potok's History of the Jews*, (New York: Fawcett Crest, 1978), p. 375.

[3] See Acts 13:50; 14:2; 14:19; 17:5f; 18:12.

[4] Josephus, *Antiquities* xx.9.1.

[5] Justin Martyr, *Dialog With Trypho* xvi.4; xlviii.5; xciii.4; xcc.4; xcvi.2; cviii.3; cxxxiii.6; cxxxvii.2.

[6] Justin Martyr, *Apology* i.31.

[7] Eusebius, *Eccl. Hist.* iv.26.3.

[8] Hippolytus, *Philos.* viii.5.18. Cited by S.L. Greenslade, *Schism in the Early Church* (London: SCM Press, Ltd., 1953), p. 26.

[9] Philip Schaff, *History of the Christian Church*, Vol. 1 (New York: Scribner, Armstrong, and Co., 1873), p. 88.

[10] Bellarmino Bagatti, *The Church From the Circumcision: History and Archaeology of the Judeo-Christians.* English Translation by Eugene Hoade (Jerusalem: Franciscan Printing Press, 1971), pp. 47-48, 87.

[11] Translation cited by Philip Schaff, *op. cit.*, p. 405. The first sentence is elsewhere translated, "Let us have nothing in common with the detestable Jewish crowd." Cited by Philip Goodman, *The Passover Anthology* (Philadelphia, The Jewish Publication Society of America, 1961), p. 16.

[12] Eusebius, *Ecclesiastical History*, "Council of Nicea" appendix. (Grand Rapids, Mich.: Baker Book House, 1955), p. 28.

[13] Bellarmino, Bagatti, *op. cit.*, p. 90.

[14] Eusebius, *op. cit.*, p. 23.

[15] *Cod. Theod.* L. 16. tit.8, 18; cf.21. Cited by Alfred Edersheim, *History of the Jewish Nation: After the Destruction of Jerusalem Under Titus* (Grand Rapids, Mich.: Baker Book House, 1895 publication republished in paperback, 1979), p. 513.

[16] Socrates, *Hist. Eccl.* vii.16. Cited by Alfred Edersheim, *op. cit.*, p. 513.

[17] Martin Luther, *Concerning the Jews and Their Lies.* Cited by Richard E. Gade, *A Historical Survey of Anti-Semitism* (Grand Rapids, Mich.: Baker Book House, 1981), p. 51.

12

WHEN I WENT FORTH FROM EGYPT

In every generation each individual is bound to regard himself as if he had gone personally from Egypt, as it is said, "And thou shalt relate to thy son on that day saying, this is on account of what the Eternal did for me, when I went forth from Egypt."

*(**Haggadah** quoting Exodus 13:8)*

People of the Jewish faith observe Passover in a ritual meal and ceremony known as a *Seder*. A book called *Haggadah Shel Pesach* (*Haggadah*, for short) contains the ceremonial procedures, readings and songs used in the Passover Seder.

Today's Jewish commemoration is not the observance instituted by the Lord through Moses, and it does not depict how Jews who accepted Jesus celebrated the passover in New Testament times.

The ceremony Jews observe today has evolved through many centuries since 70 A.D. — the Passover tradition of Rabbinical Judaism. Rabbinical Judaism refers to the Jewish tradition since the destruction of the Temple at Jerusalem in 70 A.D.

With the coming of Jesus and the destruction of the Temple shortly thereafter, Passover as observed since Moses came to an end. All Jews began to celebrate Passover in new ways.

Jews who accepted Jesus' New Covenant teaching began to celebrate Passover as fulfilled in Jesus the Messiah. They formed the foundation of what has become the predominately-Gentile Christian Church.

The majority of Jews, who did not view Jesus as the Messiah and Son of God, developed the Jewish traditions that have come to be called Rabbinical Judaism.

When the Romans destroyed the Temple at Jerusalem in 70

163

A.D., all of the animal sacrifices instituted in the Law came to an end. Jews could not observe Passover as instituted under Moses because the passover lambs, as all of the sacrifices, had to be slain at the Temple and eaten within the city of Jerusalem. Passover observance as God had commanded through Moses was no longer possible.

When Passover as commanded through Moses was no longer possible, rabbis arose to lead the Jewish people in what **was** possible (apart from accepting the New Covenant offered by Jesus.) The Jewish people could no longer offer animal sacrifices, including the Passover, that God had commanded in the Law, but they could continue to pursue the spirit of the Law. They could keep trying to be merciful and just, doing God's will with His law written in humbled and contrite hearts, working to free any bound by wickedness or any captive and oppressed.[1] At Passover time they could remember the Passover sacrifice and discuss the significance of what had occurred in the Exodus.

Within this historical and religious context they developed the Haggadah and Seder. Without the Passover sacrifice itself, the ceremony changed. The ceremony used today had only begun to take shape in the last days of the Second Temple. It arose from the teachings of the post-Temple rabbis codified in the Mishnah about 200-250 A.D. and was fixed in its final form in the tenth century.

The songs in the Haggadah date from as late as the fifteenth century. The Jewish people took to heart God's command to tell their children about His mighty acts of delivering Israel. They concluded that the telling would best be accomplished not by mere words but by that which dramatized the account. The ceremony which developed helped each person to enter his historical past and relive it with his ancestors.

Meaning of Haggadah and Seder

The Hebrew word Haggadah means, literally, a "telling" or

a "narrative." The Haggadah is a book of readings and ceremonies which, together, tell the story of the Exodus. The word Seder means "order of service," and refers to the ceremony itself which the Haggadah sets forth.

Sephardic Jews (Jews from the East and Southern Europe) have never used the term Seder. They refer to the entire Passover ritual as the Haggadah.

Development of the Haggadah as a Book

The Haggadah contains Scripture quotations, commentary by rabbis, folklore, prayers and songs. The elements of the Haggadah text span many centuries of Jewish experience and come from varied places.

The first known Haggadah for Passover appeared in a ninth century prayer book edited by a Babylonian scholar. Haggadic material for Passover remained a part of general prayer books until the 13th century when a separate Passover book was first produced.

Haggadah books were made by hand until printed Haggadahs appeared at the end of the 15th century. Whether handwritten or printed, the books were lovingly and lavishly embellished with decorations and later with illustrations.

Dating the Haggadah Material

The Scripture quotations in the Haggadah, of course, are ancient. They are the oldest material in the book. The Mishnah says that Psalms 113-118 were sung continuously by the Levites in the Temple as the passovers were sacrificed. It is not known which, if any, of the other Scriptures quoted in the Haggadah were used ritually in Passover observance before 70 A.D.

The non-Scripture Haggadah material is rooted in the *Mishnah*—the authoritative Jewish voice of rabbinical tradition codified in 200-250 A.D. The Mishnah material spans about four centuries of Jewish life in Palestine, so Jewish scholars believe it is possible some of the Passover customs mentioned in the Mishnah could date as early as the first or second century B.C. They are careful, however, not to assume any of the customs are that old, pointing out that any observance without the sacrificed passover lamb is certainly post 70 A.D.

Ceremonial customs of the Seder cannot be precisely dated. The custom of drinking four cups of wine, for example, cannot be dated with certainty before its appearance in the Mishnah.

It is known that wine, not prescribed by Moses, entered the observance at least by the time of the book of *Jubilees*, about 105 B.C. But *Jubilees* does not say how many cups were drunk. The New Testament speaks of more than one cup, but does not indicate exactly how many.

Scholars conclude from the Primary Documents that Passover observance previously was more informal and far less regulated than it is today.

There is no way of precisely dating the rabbinic commentary in the Haggadah. Rabbi Gamaliel lived at the end of the first century A.D., and Rabbi Akiva died about 135 A.D., for example, but it is not known when the quotations ascribed to them were actually written down and made part of the Passover Haggadah. One of Rabbi Akiva's prayers appears in the Haggadah just as it did in the Mishnah. Rabbi Hillel, also of the first century, is cited in the Haggadah as saying it is necessary to eat the passover lamb, and eat it with unleavened bread and bitter herbs as commanded in the Law. Yet the Haggadah proceeds on the assumption that no lamb will be eaten, and the unleavened bread and bitter herbs are eaten instead with the fruit mixture called charoset. Hillel's words about Temple time obligation were clearly set down some time after 70 A.D. and combined with the later tradition.

There are prayers throughout the Haggadah for God to rebuild Jerusalem and the Temple. These prayers, as well as the absence of the passover lamb, certainly represent a tradition developed after the 70 A.D. destruction of the Temple and the cessation of animal sacrifice.

Comparison of the Haggadah with Biblical texts confirms the Haggadah as a post-Biblical tradition. The Bible's emphasis is on the passover lamb above any other element of passover observance.

Passover was instituted as a commemoration of God's salvation of Israel from His judgment; His sparing of the first born when He saw the blood of the passover lambs upon the doors. The animal sacrifice (*pesach* in Hebrew) and the Lord's action of passing over the blood of the passover (*pasach*) is what gives the feast of Passover its name (Pesach).

The New Testament, completed in the first century A.D., carries the early emphasis on the passover lamb. First-century Jews who accepted Jesus as Messiah took the teaching of blood redemption into their theology and Passover observance. John the Baptist called Jesus "the Lamb of God who takes away the sins of the world." The Apostle John called Jesus "the Lamb slain from the foundation of the world" who has "redeemed us by His blood." Jesus, at the Last Supper Passover, took a cup of wine and said to use it to commemorate His blood shed for the remission of sins.

While the Lord instituted the Passover sacrifice to commemorate the redemption of the first born, He instituted the technically-separate Feast of Unleavened Bread to commemorate His bringing the children of Israel out of Egypt and establishing them as His holy nation. The Haggadah's emphasis on unleavened bread and national freedom (but not on blood redemption and the passover lamb) speaks of later tradition when Jews in the Diaspora could no longer sacrifice the Passover, but could observe the eating of unleavened bread.

The Seder began to take shape only in the last days of the second Temple, and was more specifically fixed in its present form in the time after the destruction of the Temple. The present ritual for Passover Eve was finally established in the tenth century.[2]

Songs appearing in a traditional Haggadah come from many eras and many places. Some are from 6th- and 7th-century Palestine; others from 14th- and 15th-century Germany.

Preparations For a Modern Seder

Jewish Passover is essentially a family observance. Preparation for Passover might begin weeks ahead as the house is thoroughly cleaned to rid it of every trace of leaven. Bread, cookies, beer, yeast, and baking powder must be discarded. Even bakers sell title to their leavened goods for the duration of the feast. (They sell it to a Gentile and purchase it back afterwards.)

The day before Passover begins the father ritually "searches" the house for any leaven. For this ceremony the mother has left a few crumbs of leaven in a conspicuous place so a prescribed prayer of disowning leaven may be pronounced concerning it. The family removes these crumbs, traditionally with a wooden spoon and feather. Then the father declares that he has rid his house of all leaven. The "discovered" and disowned leaven is ritually burned the next day.

As further preparation for Passover the family brings out special dishes and cookware used only at Passover. If the family does not own multiple sets of dishes and cookware, they must follow certain koshering (cleansing) procedures.

First-born males are expected to fast on the day before Passover as a sign of gratitude to God for delivering the first-born from the final plague in Egypt.

Tradition dictates that blessings be shared with others at Passover. Families commonly invite guests to share their Passover meal.

A holiday feast is prepared to accompany the ritual foods

eaten for Passover. The table is decorated festively and set with the best linen, china and candles.

Ritual foods are put on the ceremonial dish used in the Seder—a roasted lamb shank bone, a roasted hard-boiled egg, some parsley (or lettuce or celery), a horseradish root or other bitter herb, and a mixture of chopped apples, nuts, cinnamon, and wine.

Three pieces, or loaves, of flat unleavened bread are placed in a ceremonial cover with three "pockets," or are otherwise placed in the folds of one or two large napkins. A wine glass is set for each person and a filled wine decanter put on the table for filling them. A large glass for Elijah the prophet is placed by an empty chair at a place setting reserved for him should he come to announce Messiah's arrival that night. Dishes of salt water are placed within reach of all.

Pillows are set on the arm of the leader's chair (sometimes on everyone's chair) as a symbol of eating in ease and freedom. The participants will lean, or "recline," as a symbol of ease and freedom. A copy of the Haggadah is set by each plate. If the family is Orthodox the father will wear a long white ceremonial gown and tall white cap.

The Symbolic Foods

The ritual foods have symbolic meanings: the lamb shank bone, *z'roah*, is a reminder of the Passover Lamb. It also represents the "outstretched arm of the Lord." The egg, *baytzah*, means different things to different people. To some it represents the festival offering (the *Chaggigah*) brought to the Temple during Biblical times. To others, it is a symbol of life, or a symbol of mourning for the Temple service no longer experienced. The bitter herbs, *maror*, stand for the bitter bondage in Egypt. The apples and wine mixture, *charoset*, symbolized the mortar used by the children of Israel in slavery to the Egyptians. The greens, *karpas*, are also considered bitter herbs. And they speak of spring. The salt water into which they are dipped calls to memory the tears of the Jewish ancestors in Egypt. For some, the salt water represents the Red Sea. Some associate the greens with hyssop, and the salt water with the passover's blood into which the hyssop was dipped.

The unleavened bread, *matzah*, represents the bread baked with haste when the Israelites left Egypt in the Exodus without time for the bread to rise. It also represents the "poor bread" eaten in the Middle East—the bread of affliction in Egypt for the Israelites. Some consider the matzah a symbol of the paschal offering since 70 A.D.

Wine is a symbol of joy. The Mishnah dictates that even the poorest person in the land drink at least four cups of wine on Passover, for the Lord has commanded rejoicing at His feast.

The Passover Observance

Passover, according to the Bible, is to be celebrated on the evening of the 14th *Nisan* by the Biblical lunar calendar—still the religious calendar of the Jews. This varies from March to April on the modern solar calendar.

Orthodox and Conservative Jews have Seder services on two evenings. Reform Jews have only one. The Passover service is a night observance, with the meal eaten after nightfall. It follows a synagogue service where the Exodus narratives and other Scriptures are read and Psalms of praise are sung.

The Seder ceremony is in two parts, with the festive meal between. The family will be at the table for about three hours. There are certain places in the ritual where discussion might be interjected. Certain features, such as "the four questions," the treasure hunt for the *afikomen*, and lively songs are interjected to keep the children awake, involved, and interested.

The ceremony can be outlined around the four cups of wine

which are drunk—one cup for each of the phrases in Exodus 6:6-7, representing God's four-fold promise of redemption: (1) I will **bring you out** (2) I will **deliver you** from their bondage (3) I will **redeem you** with an outstretched arm and with great acts of judgment (4) I will **take you for my people** and I will be your God.

It has become customary to consider the cup poured for Elijah as the fifth cup referring to a fifth promise of God in Exodus 6:8: "And I will **bring you into the land** . . . [and] give it to you for a possession." For centuries Jews poured but did not drink this fifth cup, since God's promise that they would return to their homeland had not yet been fulfilled. But since 1948, when the Jews received the land of Israel as their own, many Jews have begun to drink from the Elijah cup as affirmation that the new state of Israel fulfills God's promise and marks the beginning of their redemptive period.

The First Cup: The ceremony begins with the Kiddush said by the leader. This blessing of sanctification over wine praises God the Creator for sanctifying and preserving Israel and giving His people feasts and holidays. Following this, all drink the first of the four cups of wine as they lean, or "recline."

Then there is a ritual handwashing after which the family eats of the greens dipped in salt water. Following this, the leader takes the middle of the three pieces of unleavened bread, breaks it in half, and puts one half back between the whole ones and the other half under the cloth for the *afikomen*— the last thing to be eaten that night. The *afikomen* is often hidden for the children to search for at the appropriate time. The child who finds it receives a prize.

The leader then lifts the dish with the unleavened bread and pronounces it the bread of affliction which the fathers ate in Egypt, inviting all who are hungry to celebrate and eat the Passover.

The Second Cup: The wine cups are filled the second time. Then the youngest present asks four questions about why this night is different from other nights: Why may only unleavened bread be eaten? Why must bitter herbs be eaten? Why is food ritually dipped? Why does the family recline to eat? Those present respond with readings which include references to Scripture's Exodus story and commentaries by famous rabbis. This is followed by rabbinic commentary on parts of Deuteronomy 26, Exodus 1, 3, and 12, and Joel 3.

In the song, *Dayenu* ("Enough For Us"), the family group rejoices over the many things God did for Israel, saying that each one alone would have been enough if that were all God had ever done for them.

Then attention is given to the three foods Scripture commands to be eaten at Passover: the passover lamb, the unleavened bread, and bitter herbs. The Haggadah readings recount that God commanded eating these because of what He did and said in Exodus 12.

In this portion of the Haggadah, as elsewhere, the modern Jew is bound to his peoplehood and to the Jews' entire history as he obeys the Scriptural command for each Jew in each generation to consider that he himself personally went forth from Egypt. Exodus 13:8 says "And thou shalt relate to thy son on that day saying, this is on account of what the Eternal did for **me** when **I** went forth from Egypt."

Since all have been delivered from Egypt, all are "bound to thank, praise, laud, glorify, extol, honor, bless, exalt, and reverence" the Lord for His mighty deliverance. The Haggadah, echoing the Psalms, says, "Let us therefore sing a new song in His presence. Hallelujah!"

Then the group recites or sings Psalms 113 and 114. Following this is elevation of the second cup of wine with a prayer of thanksgiving and the expressed hope that Jerusalem will be rebuilt so animal sacrifices may be resumed and the blood again sprinkled for the redemption of souls. Then the group drinks the second cup.

Again there is a ritual handwashing. The leader lifts the two and a half pieces of unleavened bread and pronounces a blessing. Then he breaks off pieces of the bread and dips these with an olive-size amount of bitter herbs into the charoset. He distributes the unleavened bread, bitter herbs and charoset to all present to eat, reading a comment about how Hillel during the existence of the Temple ate the passover lamb with unleavened bread and bitter herbs in order to perform the Law.

After the first part of the ritual the meal is served.

The Third Cup: The ceremony resumes after the meal. The group members again take up their Haggadahs and proceed.

After the meal, the *afikomen,* the matzah half put aside or hidden earlier, is brought out, broken, and distributed. All eat of it—after which no more food may be consumed that evening.

The wine cups are filled for the third time, and the family recites grace. Grace after the meal consists of several blessings, with additional prayer if Passover falls on the Sabbath.

After the blessing over the third cup, the group drinks it.

Between the drinking of the third cup and the filling of the fourth cup, the participants open their doors and quote Psalm 79:6-7, Psalm 69:25 and Lam. 3:66—imprecatory Scriptures asking God to pour out His wrath on the heathen, and to destroy in fierce anger those who have exalted themselves against Him by refusing to acknowledge His Lordship and by persecuting His chosen people Israel.

The Fourth Cup: After the fourth cup is filled, the group recites or sings Psalms 115 through 118. The Haggadah's climax follows with Psalm 136—"The Great Hallel." More praise follows, saturated with quotations from the Psalms and other

Scriptures, extolling and magnifying the Lord for His character and ways.

Three songs follow which are to be recited or sung. The first, for the first night, follows a theme of God performing many acts of deliverance in the middle of the night. The second, for the second night, has many of God's significant actions occuring on Passover. A third song, similar to a Psalm, extols God as the sovereign, omnipotent, pure, and holy ruler in His Kingdom, Who is yet a meek Redeemer.

After these songs the company recites together the prayer of hope: "The following year grant us to be in Jerusalem." Those living in Jerusalem pray to be in "Jerusalem rebuilt." Then, with a blessing, they drink the fourth cup of wine.

They offer more prayer for God to bless earthly Jerusalem and rebuild the Temple. The petition is punctuated with pleas to do so speedily.

Concluding Songs

Two lively songs conclude the Haggadah—songs that are fun for the children but which have deep meanings pertaining to the Jews. One of these is based on the thirteen basic tenants of Judaism; the other is often considered a parabolic description of historic incidents in the Jews' dispersion among the nations.

Counting the Omer

The second night of Passover includes a blessing for "Counting the Days of the *Omer*" as commanded in the Law. These are the 49 days between the Feast of Passover and the *Feast of Weeks*, also called *First Fruits, Shavuot,* and *Pentecost.*

The *omer* is an ancient measure of barley—one sheaf, or about four pints, dry measure. God commanded the people to count seven full weeks (49 days) from Passover and on the 50th day hold the feast of Weeks (Pentecost). On each of the days of counting, the ancient Israelites were to bring to the Temple an offering of their barley harvest. In this way God linked the feasts of Passover and the Feast of Weeks.

Some rabbis have calculated that the Feast of Weeks also corresponds to the giving of the Law at Sinai—50 days after the Passover in Egypt. So the Feast of Weeks has come to commemorate the Giving of the Law as well as harvest.

A Feast of Freedom

Passover is a warm family time for the Jewish people—their main occasion for family reunion. They consider it one of their most meaningful and beautiful observances. Its antiquity and universal character ties each Jew not only to his immediate family, but to all Jews everywhere in the world today. It binds him to his entire historical heritage—from the establishment of the nation of Israel under Moses, through the Golden Kingdom of David, through the persecutions of the middle ages and the 20th-century holocaust, to the refounding of the State of Israel in 1948 and the present.

As one of the most important observances of the Jewish people, Passover is discussed by poets, philosophers, scholars, and layman. Some of its specifics might mean different things to different people, but the feast overall is generally considered a celebration of national freedom. Passover in the Jewish prayer book is referred to as "the season of our freedom."

Footnotes:
[1]Hosea 6:6; Prov. 21:3; Ps. 40:6-8;Ps. 51:16-17; Is. 58:1-7
[2]Chaim Raphael, *A Feast of History* (New York: Simon & Schuster, 1972), pp. 67-80.

13

NEXT YEAR IN JERUSALEM

*...come and celebrate the Passover. At present we
celebrate it here, but next year we hope to celebrate it in
the land of Israel. This year we are servents here, but
next year we hope to be freemen in the land of
Israel... The following year grant us to be in Jerusalem.*
(Haggadah)

Judaism's Passover observance looks not only to the past
but also to the present and future. Beyond commemorating
deliverance in ancient Egypt the Haggadah expresses Messianic
hope and expectation. Woven into its tapestry are prayers and
longings that God would continue to deliver, save and redeem.

In order to understand the Haggadah's specific expressions
about salvation and redemption, it is necessary to look first
at some general differences between Christianity and Judaism.
The two religions have different meanings for some of the same
words. It is also helpful to remember that the Haggadah, span-
ning many centuries, includes some older Jewish thinking that
doesn't represent the beliefs of many modern Jews. Salvation,
redemption and Messiah have meant different things to Christians, ancient Jews and modern Jews. The Christian can't read
his own definitions into the language and meaning of the
Haggadah.

Christian Definitions

Christians believe that the Messiah has come in the person
of Jesus. To Christians with a New Testament perspective the
salvation and redemption that Messiah brings has to do with
freeing the soul from sin as well as freeing the body from earth's
ills. Christians believe Messiah Jesus has brought God's King-

dom of righteousness within the hearts of men, paving the way for His coming in glory as King to raise the dead and to redeem the rest of the physical world, establishing an eternal kingdom on a recreated earth.

Jewish Belief About Messiah and the Messianic Age

The vast majority of Jews today believe in a coming Messianic age but many question whether this age will be ushered in by a person. Orthodox Jews and many Conservative Jews look for a personal Messiah, while Reformed Jews believe in a Messianic age without any personal Messiah.

Jews believe Jesus was not the Messiah because he did not usher in the Messianic age of peace on earth. They deny that Jesus rose from the dead, and believe that if he had truly been the Messiah he would not have died in the first place. Christians, they believe, conjured up the resurrection and second coming teachings when Jesus did not deliver what Messiah was prophesied to bring. The Talmud does not deny the miracles of Jesus but attributes them to magic and sorcery. Jews reject Jesus' claim of divinity as blasphemous.

There have been different times in history when Jews have followed men who they thought at first was the Messiah, but who they later rejected as a false Messiah. Jesus is considered to be one of those pseudo-Messiahs.

The Messianic age will be a time when there will be peace on earth—no war, no hatred, no killing. Mankind's suffering will be alleviated.

Exodus and Sinai are considered models of salvation in the Messianic era. Israel experienced physical redemption in their delivery from slavery in Egypt, and spiritual redemption in their covenant with God and the giving of the Law at Sinai. The Messianic age will be a time of physical deliverance from the world's ills and spiritual redemption in that the world's people will together acknowledge that there is one Lord in the earth, and His name is one.

Jews do not believe in sitting and waiting for Messiah to come. They believe that sanctification involves both prayer and action. Many believe that man's actions can hasten or delay the coming of Messiah. Some believe that Messiah will come either when all men become righteous enough or when all men become sinners needing outside redemption. Unlike Christians who feel complete in individual salvation, Jews think of salvation in terms of the whole earth; they do not feel complete as long as the world remains unredeemed. They strive toward personal/world redemption through prayer, Torah study, and good deeds. They work to bring the Messiah.

Jewish Beliefs About Salvation and Redemption

Jews tend to place far less emphasis than Christians on matters such as heaven and hell, life after death, and resurrection of the body. Instead, they emphasize redeeming the world through social action, etc. They feel Christians have spiritualized Biblical teaching about Messiah and Passover, severing the Biblical concepts from the material context in which they were given. While many Christians, notably Evangelicals, tend to put heaviest emphasis on redemption of the individual soul and spirit, Jews tend to put heaviest emphasis on the redemption of the world.

Jews do not share the Christian belief that blood atonement and individual salvation is the means by which the world will be redeemed. Jews today believe that even in the days before the destruction of the Temple, when animal sacrifice was still practiced, salvation was not reduced to only blood atonement. God always wanted sacrifice accompanied by a heart that was right toward Him or the sacrifice meant nothing. Today sacrifice is no longer possible, but prayer is.

Jews do not feel the need for blood atonement that Christians do because they do not share the same belief as Christians that man is a fallen creation with a sinful nature.

Judaism today does not subscribe to a fall from God's grace (original sin). It teaches that man's soul, which came from a pure God, is inherently pure and good. Sin, by Judaism's definition, is not a soul condition but a specific action in which one does not live up to his full potential.

Sin is atoned for, according to Rabbinical Judaism, not by any vicarious blood sacrifice, but by honest soul searching, admitting to the shortcoming, turning around and not repeating the failure, winning the forgiveness of the person who has been wronged, and firmly resolving to do better in the future.

Messianic Hope Expressed in the Haggadah

There is a prayer in the Haggadah expressing Jewish thinking about receiving righteousness from God and mercifully being made worthy by Him, and about this salvation having to do with a personal Messiah:

> *May we receive a blessing from the Lord,*
> *and righteousness from the God of our*
> *salvation . . . may He who is most merciful*
> *cause us to inherit the day that is entirely*
> *good. May He who is most merciful make us*
> *worthy to behold the day of the Messiah and*
> *eternal life in the future state. He giveth*
> *great salvation to his King, and showeth*
> *mercy to his Anointed; to David, and his seed*
> *forever. May He who maketh peace in his high*
> *heavens grant peace unto us, and all Israel,*
> *and let us say, Amen.*

Most of the concern, however, is for deliverance from mortal ills unto temporal welfare.

> *Deliver us speedily from all our troubles; and suffer*
> *us not, Eternal, our God, to stand in need of the*
> *gifts of mankind, nor their loan; but let us depend*

on thy full, open, holy, and extensive hand,
so that we may not be put to shame , nor ever
be confounded.

. . . and may we never lack any good thing.

May He who is most merciful, maintain us with
honor. May He who is most merciful break the yoke
of captivity from off our neck, and lead us securely
to our land. May He who is most merciful, send us
abundant blessings in this house, and on this table
on which we have eaten. May He who is most
merciful, send us Elijah the prophet of blessed
memory, to bring us the good tidings of salvation
and consolation.

O Lord, our God, remember us this day for good,
visit us with thy blessing and save us to enjoy life.

. . . and in thy good will, suffer no trouble, sorrow,
or affliction, to affect us on our day of rest.

Some modern Jews have adopted the custom of setting aside an empty chair or cup of wine as a symbol of their incompleteness so long as Jews in Russia have no religious feedom to celebrate Passover with them. Prayers of concern for Jews trapped in the Soviet Union unite the cries of the Israelites under Egyptian bondage with those of their twentieth century brethren. To Jews who take seriously the teaching that they should actively work for the freedom of any enslaved or oppressed people, Passover is a time of inspiration and resolve to remember others presently oppressed under political tyranny, poverty, hunger or any other bitter yoke.

Concern for mortal welfare is at the heart of the salvation longed for in the expressions of Messianic hope in the Haggadah. Such salvation had come to be thought of by the Haggadah writers as possible and permanent for the Jew only in his ancient homeland.

Hope for the Homeland

The Haggadah's beginning paragraphs contain the united prayer of a dispersed and persecuted people longing for their homeland:

> *At present we celebrate it here, but next year*
> *we hope to celebrate it in the land of Israel.*
> *This year we are servants here, but next year*
> *we hope to be freemen in the land of Israel.*

The hope for the homeland is expressed elsewhere in the Haggadah as well:

> *May He who is most merciful break the yoke of*
> *captivity from off our neck, and lead us securely*
> *to our land.*

Since the restoration of the state of Israel in 1948 Jews have had opportunity to experience the return to their land, fulfilling their centuries-old Messianic hopes. Mere residence in the land of Israel does not give a sense of ultimate freedom and salvation, however. Great numbers of Jews have not chosen the salvation of immigrating there and those already in the land make a further plea: "Next year in Jerusalem rebuilt." Restoration of Israel marks only the beginning of the Messianic age.

The Haggadah's blessing over the third cup specifies that "Jerusalem rebuilt" refers to a rebuilt Temple and the restoration of animal sacrifices:

> *Mayest thou bring us to enjoy in peace other solemn*
> *feasts and sacred seasons, which approach us, that*
> *we may rejoice in the building of thy city and exult*
> *in the holy service; that we may there eat of the*
> *sacrifices of the holy paschal offerings, whose blood*
> *shall be sprinkled upon the side of thine altar,*
> *for thine acceptance. Then shall we, with a new*
> *hymn, give thanks to Thee for our deliverance, and*
> *for the redemption of our souls.*

14

CHRIST IN THE PASSOVER

In the middle matzah we see Christ in the Passover—the Second Person of the Godhead, whose body was pierced in death, hidden away in the tomb, and brought forth again in His resurrection.
(From a Messianic Jewish Seder presentation to Gentiles)

The twentieth century has produced something the world has not seen for over 1,500 years—large numbers of Jews accepting Jesus as Messiah. These new Jewish Christians are not all alike in expression of their faith. They do not all have the same systematic theology. They do not all espouse the same ideas about worship services or sharing their faith. Some have been greatly influenced by the charismatic movement; others have not.

One thing that characterizes the great majority of the Jewish Christians is the belief that Passover should be celebrated in a way that commemorates both God's deliverance of Israel in the Exodus, and the redemption in Jesus which that original Passover event also foreshadows. Perhaps for many the desire to celebrate Passover is as much a desire to retain ties to their Jewish peoplehood and to continue a beloved tradition as it is to show forth certain truths ritually.

From the twentieth century Jewish Christian movement to celebrate Passover—still in its infancy; still in a state of flux—there has emerged so far one type of service known generally as a "Messianic Jewish Seder." Messianic seders vary, but nearly always have a seder plate and include some usage of the Haggadah, along with other material.

Messianic Jews see Christ not only in the Bible's Passover symbolism, but also in Rabbinical Judaism's Passover symbolism. They see Him in the Bible's passover lamb and unleavened bread. They also see Him in the ritual foods on the seder plate. He is the lamb represented by the shankbone. The egg, representing another Temple offering, also symbolizes Jesus who fulfills all animal sacrifice. The greens are fulfilled in Messiah who is the Life—in whom is all springtime newness, physical and spiritual. The three matzot in the folds of the one cloth represent God the Father, Son, and Spirit in composite unity. The breaking of the middle matzah symbolizes Messiah the Son's death; its hiding away, His burial; its bringing out again, His resurrection.

In a Messianic seder, the participants use the traditional Jewish Haggadah in some way. Some read it as is, simply overlooking the Rabbinical Jewish theology in which it was written, interpreting its prayers for salvation according to their own theology. Others alter the Haggadah and add to it to bring it fully in line with belief about Jesus being Messiah. Still others write their own Haggadah patterned after the traditional Haggadah. They incorporate elements from the Haggadah, elements from Christian tradition, and newly composed material.

In celebrating Jesus' redemption being the fulfillment of Passover, Jewish believers add Scripture readings about spiritual salvation to their seders. They sing the joyful music of those who have found the Messiah and eternal life.

THE PASSOVER PRIMARY DOCUMENTS

When scolars make a thorough study of Passover as it was observed before the destruction of the Temple in 70 A.D., they consult the existing writings that date from before 70 A.D. There are only a few of these extant "primary documents," as they are called.

Writings which were completed after 70 A.D. are called "secondary sources." There are not as valuable, reliable, or authoratative as the primary documents for understanding how Passover was observed at the time of Christ and before the Temple was destroyed. The Mishnah of 200 A.D., and then the Talmud of a much later date are secondary sources for understanding how Passover was observed in the Bible and for understanding the Passover context of the Last Supper.

The Bible itself is the chief of the primary documents in that it contains the most information—not to mention it being the authoritative Word of God. The non-Biblical primary documents tell very little about Passover observance that is not already in the Bible.

The Passover primary documents are:
- the Bible—Old Testament and New Testament
- the Elephantine documents
- the Qumran documents
- the Greek tragedy by Ezekielos
- the pseudepigraphal books
- the *Megillath Ta'anith*
- the writings of Philo
- the writings of Josephus

Laymen as well as scholars can benefit from knowledge of the primary documents. When someone presents them with a statement that "this is how Passover was observed at the Last Supper," for example, they know where to look to check the facts. Books such as J.B. Segal's *The Hebrew Passover From the Earliest Times to 70 A.D.* and Philip Goodman's *The Passover Anthology* contain the complete translated texts of all primary documents, with explanatory comments. An introductory summary of each of the Primary Documents follows.

The Bible

Those who consider the Bible the Word of God put it in a class by itself. It is **the** authority for Passover as well as for every other subject on which God has spoken. All other writings are subordinate to the Bible. The Bible is not interpreted by other documents; it interprets them. The Lord instituted Passover; therefore, His Word best discusses it.

Sometimes other writings give historical and cultural details that the Bible does not give and thereby complement the Biblical narratives. But whenever another source contradicts the Bible, the Bible's word is taken as the authoritative word.

The Bible is not only the authoritative Word of God in matters of Passover theology, it is the richest source for historical and cultural details about Passover observance. Bible references to Passover have been cited and discussed in the first nine chapters.

The Elephantine Documents

The Elephantine documents consist of three brief fragments, all in Aramaic, which are named for the place in which they were discovered in 1905—Elephantine in Upper Egypt. They date to the fifth century B.C., about the time of the book Ezra. Two of these are written on potsherds (pieces of broken pottery called "ostraca") and one is on papyrus.

Elephantine is a small island in the upper Nile, opposite Aswan. A military post was established there around 588-569 B.C. Under Darius II, King of Persia from 424-404 B.C., Elephantine was the location of the garrison of Jewish soldiers in the Persian army serving as guards near the Egyptian border. These were Jews who did not return from the Babylonian exile to Palestine under Ezra and Nehemiah after Cyrus overthrew Babylon in 539 B.C. These half-assimilated mercenaries looked to Palestine for guidance, but did not completely know or follow the Jewish law. For example, they were one of three Jewish communities which had its own temple contrary to Biblical commands concerning the one Temple in Jerusalem.

The ostraca fragments each have parts of a couple sentences. (One has about 10 words of English translation; the other has about 20 words.) One ostracon, ascribed to the earlier half of the fifth century B.C., is from one person or group to another and contains the words "on the Passover" and "examining his vessels." The other ostracon, ascribed to 500 B.C., is apparently a letter sent by a Jewish soldier as a request for someone to write and tell him when that person would "make the Passover."

The importance of the two ostraca is that they show Passover and the Feast of Unleavened Bread to be of interest to the Elephantine Jews. However, they give no details beyond the Bible record about how ancient Jews celebrated the two institutions.

The Elephantine papyrus is dated within its text in the fifth year of Darius (Darius II, King of Persia—419 B.C.) It is a letter from one Hananiah to Yadoniah and his collegues, the Jewish garrison at Elephantine. It contains about 120 words (English translation) of broken words and sentences. It refers to a decree sent from Darius to Arsames, Persian governor of Egypt, regarding the Jewish observance of eating unleavened foods during the seven days observance of the Feast of Unleavened

Bread which began the day the Passover was eaten. There is no reference to the Passover in this papyrus. Its contents have to do with being ritually clean, not eating or drinking anything with leaven, not having leaven in one's chambers, and not working (presumably on feast days).

The Qumran Documents

Qumran is a region in Northwest Jordan near the northwest shore of the Dead Sea. It is the site of the caves in which the Dead Sea Scrolls have been found. It was undoubtedly the center of the Jewish sect known as Essenes.

The founding of Qumran probably dates back to the time of the Maccabees. Coins found there begin at the time of the reign of John Hyrcanus (135-104 B.C.) An earthquake caused evacuation for about 25 years, from about 31 B.C. to 4 B.C. In 68 A.D. Vespasian entered the Dead Sea region with the Roman Tenth Legion and took the Qumran community by assault. The ruins were again occupied from 68-132 A.D., until the second Jewish rebellion under Bar Kochba.

This community's written documents and archaeological remains do not contribute any new information about Passover. Their apocryphal and sectarian texts do not mention Passover. No altar has been discovered there. It is believed, therefore, that they either repudiated animal sacrifice or followed the Biblical command restricting sacrifice to the Temple in Jerusalem. Thus, they would not have observed Passover as in the Bible.

The Qumran documents on Passover are fragments of the Bible written in Hebrew. Some are on parchment.

Ezekielos

Ezekielos is not to be confused with the prophet Ezekiel who wrote the Bible book bearing his name. This Ezekielos (also called Ezekiel) was a Hellenist Jewish dramatist who lived in Alexandria, Egypt in the second century B.C. He composed a tragedy in Greek entitled *The Exodus From Egypt.*

In this poetic drama he repeats in his own words, with expansion, the Biblical account in Exodus 12 and 13. He evidently knew the Biblical texts from the Septuagint (a Greek translation of the Hebrew Bible made by Jews in Alexandria which includes the additional books known as the Apocrypha.)

Although Ezekielos follows the Biblical accounts closely, there are significant omissions in his listing of laws regarding Passover observance. He omits the laws that circumcision was a prerequisite for observance, that bitter herbs must be eaten with the Passover lamb, and that the Passover meal was to be eaten in family units.

Most probably, Ezekielos' non-Palestinian audience observed only the Feast of Unleavened Bread and not the Passover. His poetic work included details of historical and dramatic interest, not details given as guidelines for observance. The Hellenist Jews in Alexandria and Gentiles who were his audience would not be observing Passover.

The Pseudepigraphal Books—*Jubilees*

Pseudepigrapha means "having a false title." The term refers to a group of early writings (between 200 B.C. and 150 A.D.), some of which were falsely ascribed to Biblical personages. These were written mostly in Hebrew and Aramaic, but some were in Greek. They were not given official recognition by the Jewish authorities or included in the Biblical canon.

Jubilees, one of the pseudepigraphal books, was written in Palestine in the second century B.C. between 135-105 B.C. — probably just before 105 B.C. It was written in Greek, but is extant in its entirety only in an Ethiopic version which is a translation of the Greek. The book purports to be the secrets revealed to Moses by an angel. The subject matter covers

Hebrew history from Creation to the Giving of the Law at Sinai. The author retells the Biblical account in his own words adding to or omitting from Genesis and Exodus as he chooses. Running through the book is the theme of the jubilee of years. A jubilee was 49 years divided into "weeks"—periods of seven years.

Some scholars think the author of *Jubilees* was a Pharisee. Others point to the solar calendar around which the book is constructed (which varies from normative Judaism) and conclude the author was a member of a heterodox sect.

Chapters 48 and 49 of *Jubilees* have reference to the Exodus from Egypt. Chapter 48 does not mention Passover. Chapter 49, based on Exodus 12, gives a detailed description of Passover. The author emphasizes the offering of the passover lamb, placing the sacrifice between 2 p.m. and 6 p.m. The lamb had to be sacrificed at the Temple and the ritual meal eaten in the Temple courts before 2:00 a.m. The author does not mention the bitter herbs or unleavened bread.

Jubilees speaks of the Passover participants "drinking the wine" and "lauding and blessing and giving thanks to the Lord God of their fathers." The book depicts Passover as a joyful, informal family festival. The details of observance agree with the Old Testament accounts except for the drinking of wine which is not mentioned in the Old Testament. It is first mentioned in *Jubilees*. It is not specified how many cups of wine the participants drink.

The Pseudepigraphal Books—
The Wisdom of Solomon

The Wisdom of Solomon was not written by Solomon. It was written in Greek between 50 B.C. and 10 A.D. by a writer generally supposed to have been an Alexandrian Jew or possibly a Palestinian Jew.

The book is didactic and philosophical in nature, written around the theme of God's wisdom seen in the Exodus. There are no direct references to Passover observance in the book, but some see a brief allusion to Passover in chapter 18, verse 9. This speaks of "holy children of good men offering sacrifice in secret, and with one consent taking upon themselves the covenant of the divine law," mentioning that they were "singing the while the fathers' songs of praise."

The Wisdom of Solomon appears in the Catholic Bible. It has 19 chapters praising wisdom, the last 10 concerning the wisdom of God in the Exodus event. It is similar in style to Proverbs and Ecclesiastes. Paul and other New Testament writers give evidence of acquaintance with it.

Megillath Ta'anith

Megillath Ta'anith is a tractate, or treatise, from the *Talmud*. The *Talmud* is the collection of writings constituting the Jewish civil and religious law. It has two parts: the *Mishnah* (text) and the *Gemara* (commentary on the text). The *Mishnah* text is a collection of rabbinic commentary on the Scripture. It was codified in 200 A.D. It includes some oral tradition which scholars say might go back as far as the second century B.C. *Megillath Ta'anith* dates from before 66 A.D.

Written in Aramaic, the brief passage in *Megillath Ta'anith* which concerns Passover has to do with purification rites before Passover. The passage speaks of the "second Pesach" of the Bible—Passover observance a month late for those unable to observe in the month of Nisan due to ritual uncleanness, mourning, or absence in a distant country. The text states that the celebration is to be joyful. No fasting or mourning is allowed.

Philo

Philo Judaeus (c. 20 B.C.-c. 40 A.D.) lived in Alexandria, Egypt, a contemporary of Jesus. As a resident of Alexandria he was greatly influenced by Greek philosophy. This is reflected in his writings which blend Greek philosophy with Biblical revelation. Philo wrote in Greek. Most of his works are preserved in the Greek; a few survive in Armenian translation.

He made broad use of allegory in his writings. Repetition, tangents, and no systematic organization of ideas characterize his style.

Philo's works contain scattered references to Passover, but they do not give full or precise details of ritual. For example, Philo writes that laymen acted as priests in slaughtering the Passover lambs, but he does not mention the priests' handling of the blood, which could lead to the erroneous conclusion that laymen acted as priests in all matters of the Passover sacrifice.

He is the first writer to make significance out of Passover coming at the spring equinox. He associates spring and Passover with the Creation.

Philo says little more about Passover than what is in the Bible. His descriptions of Passover are descriptions of others observing the Feast in Jerusalem. He and his countrymen in Alexandria did not celebrate the Feast there.

There is a treatise, *Questions and Answers to Genesis and Exodus*, which is ascribed to Philo (although not with certainty). The only surviving complete manuscript is in Armenian. If it was not written by Philo, it seems at least to be from his period. This treatise enumerates individual ceremonies of Passover, and gives the author's allegorical explanations. According to this manuscript, Passover was the festival of "passing over," and the regulations enumerated coincide with the Biblical regulations.

The treatise mentions Biblical Passover regulations which had been changed or abandoned. At the time of Philo (or the other writer of the treatise,) the lamb was no longer selected on the 10th day and kept until the 14th, the blood of the lamb was no longer put on the door, the participants no longer dressed as though for quick departure, and the remains of the lamb were no longer burned at dawn. The regulation about the addition of neighbors to a small family was modified. It seems that the required age of the lamb, the conditions pertaining to its roasting, and the rule about eating it only at night had also been modified—perhaps because of the great numbers of pilgrims who crowded Jerusalem to participate in the celebrations.

Josephus

Flavius Josephus was a Jewish historian and soldier who lived about 37 A.D. to 100 A.D. He was a member of a noble family and a Pharisee. He served as an interpreter for Vespasian and Titus and was an intermediary between Romans and Jews. After the fall of Jerusalem in 70 A.D. he went to Rome where he was granted Roman citizenship. His writings include his autobiography and his major works: *The Antiquities of the Jews*, *The Wars of the Jews*, and *Against Apion*. His historical data at times contradicts Scripture's historical record.

When Josephus wrote about the Passover ritual he referred to the festival as "Pascha"; when he wrote of Passover week he called the entire week "the Feast of the Unleavened Bread." In one place he referred to the entire week (including the first-day Passover ceremony) as "the Feast of Unleavened Bread which is called the Pascha."

Josephus adds commentary and personal views about the eating of unleavened bread which contradict Biblical statements.

He describes the offerings of barley which begin on the second day of the Festival of Unleavened Bread, and records that the Feast of Weeks (the fiftieth day after the barley sheaf offering) was then called *Asarta*.

According to Josephus the pilgrims arrived in Jerusalem on the 8th of Nisan. Foreigners and those ritually unclean could not participate. His estimate of those participating in the

Passover observances of 65 and 70 A.D. was about three million, a number which is probably much exaggerated but which communicates a scene of extreme crowdedness.

He records that the people ate the Passover in units called *fratria*—normally between ten and twenty persons. The Passover lambs in Josephus' day were slain in the Temple between 3 and 5 p.m. and were eaten in houses within the city. Just after midnight the priests reopened the Temple gates.

THE SAMARITAN
PASSOVER OBSERVANCE

When the ten northern tribes of Israel were defeated by Sargon of Assyria and went into captivity in 722 B.C. some of the Israelites remained in the land in cities such as Samaria, Shiloh and Shechem, located west of the Jordan River about half way between the Sea of Galilee and the Dead Sea. These Israelites intermarried with the defeated people from other nations who Sargon resettled in Israel. The mixed race which resulted also had a mixed religion, worshipping pagan gods as well as the Lord. They came to be called Samaritans. The Samaritan religion included the Pentateuch of Moses, but not the writings of the prophets or other Biblical writings.

In later years when the Jews of the Southern Kingdom were returning to the land from their captivity, they excluded the Samaritans from participation in rebuilding the Temple under Nehemiah because of their racial and religious impurity. In Nehemiah's day a number of dissident Jews emigrated to the country of the Samaritans. Manasseh, son-in-law of Sanballat who opposed Nehemiah's work, was one of those dissidents who went to Samaria. While there, he convinced the Samaritans to leave many of their idolatrous customs. Then the Samaritans and the assimilated dissidents built their own temple on Mount Gerizim near Shechem. That temple was destroyed in 109 B.C., but the Samaritans continued to worship and observe Passover on Mount Gerizim.

By the time of Christ the entire region encompassing the cities of Samaria, Shiloh and Shechem was named Samaria. It lay between Galilee and Judea. The discussion between

Jesus and the Samaritan woman at the well brings out some of the differences between the Samaritan sect and mainline Judaism. The Jews followed the Bible's instructions to worship only at the Temple He placed on Mount Zion. They also had more complete revelation because they had the prophets as well as the Law.

The Samaritan sect has continued to the present. They still worship on Mt. Gerizim. Their priest leaders are based in the nearby city of Nablus. The Samaritans continue to celebrate Passover as described in the Pentateuch.

They select lambs or goats according to the Law of Moses, roast them in primitive ovens, eat them with unleavened bread and bitter herbs, and follow the other rules prescribed in the five books of Moses. Through Moses, God had commanded only that the passovers be slain and eaten in the place where He "put His name." In Moses' time, and in the following centuries until David brought the tabernacle to Jerusalem, the place where God put His name changed. The Samaritans, not having the Scripture after Moses, believe Mt. Gerizim (the place their spiritual fathers selected) is the holy place of worship.

According to later Scripture, God designated Jerusalem as the one place for Jewish worship. The Temple was built there. No other place was acceptable for sacrifice and worship. The passover lambs had to be slain at the Temple on Mt. Zion, Jerusalem. Because of this, the Jews do not celebrate Passover as the Samaritans do. The Jerusalem Temple was destroyed in 70 A.D. Even though Jews now politically control the Temple mount they cannot build a new temple and reinstate animal sacrifice: a Moslem mosque occupies the site of the Temple. But the majority of Jews today have come to think of sacrificing animals as obsolete. They would not want to celebrate Passover as the Samaritans do— as they once did.

THE SO-CALLED "GOSPELS' PASSOVER DISCREPANCIES"

Several Passover references in the Gospel of John raise questions about the chronology of the Last Supper and Jesus' crucifixion. Some Bible commentators believe there are discrepancies between John's chronology and the other Gospels' chronology. As they see it, John says Jesus was crucified **before** the passover was eaten, which puts him in contradiction to Matthew, Mark, and Luke who tell of Jesus being crucified **after** the passover was eaten.

But John's Gospel does not contradict the other Gospels. That thesis is presented in three steps. First, it is pointed out that the Synoptic writers (Matthew, Mark, and Luke) clearly say the Last Supper they describe is a Passover meal. Second it is demonstrated that the supper John speaks of is the same meal as that in the Synoptic Gospels, and is therefore the Passover. Third, each Passover reference in John's Gospel is discussed individually with information showing it does not contradict the other Gospels.

Some Bible critics say that none of the Gospels' Last Supper accounts refer to the Passover meal. They say certain other Passover references in all the Gospels would be in contradiction to the Law if the Last Supper were the Passover. The Passover references upon which their viewpoint is based are also discussed here.

The Synoptics' Meal Was the Passover

The Last Supper accounts in Matthew, Mark, and Luke all

196

state clearly within the text that the meal spoken of was the Passover:

> *Now the first day of the feast of unleavened bread*
> *the disciples came to Jesus, saying unto him, Where*
> *will thou that we prepare for thee to eat the*
> *passover?. . . And he said, Go into the city to such a*
> *man, and say unto him, The Master saith, My time*
> *is at hand; I will keep the passover at thy house with*
> *my disciples. And the disciples did as Jesus had*
> *appointed them; and they made ready the passover.*
> *Now when even was come, he sat down with the*
> *twelve. And as they did eat. . .*　　　*(Matt. 26:17-21)*

> *And the first day of unleavened bread, when they*
> *killed the passover, his disciples said unto him,*
> *Where wilt thou that we go and prepare that thou*
> *mayest eat the passover? And he sendeth forth two of*
> *his disciples, and saith unto them, Go ye into the*
> *city, and there shall meet you a man. . . and*
> *wheresoever he shall go in, say ye to the goodman of*
> *the house, The Master saith, Where is the guest*
> *chamber where I shall eat the passover with my*
> *disciples? And he will shew you a large upper room*
> *furnished and prepared: there make ready for*
> *us. . . and they made ready the passover. And in the*
> *evening he cometh with the twelve. And as they sat*
> *and did eat. . .*　　　*(Mk. 14:12-18)*

> *Then came the day of unleavened bread, when the*
> *passover must be killed. And he sent Peter and John,*
> *saying, Go and prepare us the passover, that we*
> *may eat. . . and they made ready the passover. And*
> *when the hour was come, he sat down, and the*
> *twelve apostles with him. And he said unto them,*
> *With desire I have desired to eat this passover with*
> *you before I suffer.*　　　*(Lk. 22:7-15)*

These passages indicate, moreover, that Jesus and His

disciples observed Passover at the same time as all others in the Jewish nation. This is evident from that statements that they observed it when the passover "**must** be killed" and when "**they**" (the Jews in general) observed it (Matt., 26:17; Mk. 14:12; Lk. 22:7). Jesus did not observe Passover before the 14th Nisan using sectarian guidelines or a different calendar.

John's Meal Was the Passover

Unlike the Synoptic Gospel writers, John does not state that the meal he describes is the Passover. And he does not record a great body of material about that meal in common with the three synoptic Gospels. But he does have certain narratives in common with the synoptics which are of such a nature as to indicate that he is speaking of the same meal. These common narratives include Jesus foretelling Judas's betrayal, Jesus foretelling Peter's denial, and the leaving for the garden where Jesus shortly thereafter was arrested. A comparison of these accounts follows:

Jesus Foretells Betrayal by Judas

J   Verily, verily, I say unto you that one of you will betray me. (Jn. 13:21)

Mk Verily, I say unto you, that one of you shall betray me. (Matt. 26:21)

Mk Verily I say unto you, One of you which eateth with me shall betray me. (Mk. 14:18)

L   But, behold, the hand of him that betrayeth me is with me on the table. (Lk. 22:21)

The Disciples' Response

J   ...the disciples looked one on another, doubting of whom he spoke...Lord, who is it? (Jn. 13:22.25)

M   ...began every one of them to say unto him, Lord, is it I? (Matt. 26:22)

Mk ...began...to say to Him one by one, Is it I?...Is it I? (Mk. 14:19)

L They began to inquire among themselves, which of them it was that should do this thing. (Lk. 22:23)

The Sign of the Sop

J Jesus answered, He it is, to whom I shall give a sop, when I have dipped it. And when he had dipped the sop, he gave it to Judas. (Jn. 13:26)

M He answered and said, He that dippeth his hand with me in the dish. (Matt. 26:23)

Mk He answered and said unto them, It is one of the twelve that dippeth with me in the dish. (Mk. 14:20)

L ——

Peter's Declaration of Loyalty

J Peter said unto him...I will lay down my life for thy sake... (Jn. 13:37)

M Peter answered and said...yet will I never be offended... Though I should die with thee, yet will I not deny thee. (Matt. 26:33,35)

Mk Peter said unto him, Although all shall be offended, yet will not I...If I should die with thee, I will not deny thee in any wise. (Mk. 14:29, 31)

L He said unto him, Lord I am ready to go with thee, both into prison, and to death. (Lk. 22:33)

Jesus Foretells Peter's Denial

J Jesus answered him, Wilt thou lay down thy life for my sake? Verily, verily, I say unto thee, The cock shall not crow, till thou has denied me thrice. (Jn. 13:38)

M Jesus said unto him, Verily, I say unto thee, That this night, before the cock crow, thou shalt deny me thrice. (Matt. 26:34)

Mk Jesus saith unto him, Verily I say unto thee, That this day, even in this night, before the cock crows twice, thou shalt deny me thrice. (Mk. 14:30)

L And he said, I tell thee, Peter, the cock shall not crow this day, before that thou shalt thrice deny that thou knowest me. (Lk. 22:34)

Out to the Garden

J He went forth with his disciples over the brook Cedron, where was a garden, into the which he entered, and his disciples. (Jn. 18:1)

M ...they went out into the Mount of Olives...unto a place called Gethsemane. (Matt. 26:30, 36)

Mk ...they went out into the Mount of Olives...to a place which was named Gethsemane. (Mk. 14:26, 32)

L He came out, and went...to the Mount of Olives, and his disciples also followed him. (Lk. 22:39)

It is possible, but highly unlikely, that Jesus would have at two separate meals predicted Judas's betrayal and each time accompanied the prediction with the sign of the sop. It is not plausible that Judas would have come back to the group, once he had been exposed as the betrayer. The passages about Judas's predicted betrayal, accompanied by the sign of the sop, could only refer in all four Gospels to the same incident at the same meal. To conclude that this same incident happened twice at two different meals is a forced and unnatural interpretation.

Similarly, it is highly unlikely—in fact it is nearly inconceivable, that Jesus would have on two separate occasions predicted Peter's denial—each time at a meal, each time with Peter emphatically declaring he would die for Jesus rather than deny Him, and each time Jesus responding to Peter's declaration of loyalty by saying Peter would deny Him that very night before the cock crowed.

Finally, in John's Gospel, as well as in the other three, Jesus and His disciples left the meal under discussion and went to the garden where Jesus was arrested and soon thereafter crucified.

All four Gospels are discussing the same meal—the Last Supper Passover meal on the night in which Jesus was betrayed and arrested in the garden.

John's Passover Chronology

It is evident that John and the Synoptic writers wrote of the same Last Supper Passover meal. There is no indication, as is sometimes maintained, that John wrote intending to "correct erroneous chronology" in Matthew, Mark, and Luke. Each of John's Passover references must be considered individually. A correct understanding of each reference is needed to determine whether John and the other Gospels are unintentionally in contradiction to each other, or whether their narratives jibe.

John 13:1—"before the feast":

> *Now before the feast of the passover, when Jesus knew that his hour was come that he should depart out of this world unto the Father, having loved his own which were in the world, he loved them unto the end.*

This verse has a complicated construction. It raises the question, "To what does the phrase 'before the feast' refer?"

Some say it might refer to all of the narrative which follows in the next several chapters about a meal Jesus ate with His disciples. Disregarding the supper narratives John has in common with the Synoptic Gospels which say the supper was the Passover, they conclude that the meal in John's Gospel was not the Passover. They build a theory upon an unclear verse, disregarding the principle of sound Biblical interpretation that says unclear verses much be interpreted in light of clear verses.

Others say the phrase "before the feast" has to do with the next phrase in the sentence about Jesus knowing that the time of His departure from this world had come; both phrases pertain to the final words in the sentence about Jesus continuing to love His disciples until the end of His life on earth. Before the Feast of Passover, Jesus knew He was about to be arrested and killed. He knew that one of His own disciples would betray Him, one would deny Him, and all would desert Him. Even so, He continued to love them to the end of His life on earth just as He loved them before the coming of Passover. His love was demonstrated in His Last Supper with them when He washed their feet, encouraged them, and told them about the Comforter, and so on.

John 19:14—"the preparation"

> *And it was the preparation of the passover, and about the sixth hour: and he [Pilate] saith unto the Jews, Behold your King!*

Since preparing for an event precedes the event, the expression "preparation of the passover" raises the question of whether or not the passover meal was yet future at this point in John's narrative. The question must be answered with a correct understanding of what "the Preparation" means. It is a term used elsewhere.

"Preparation of the Sabbath" or simply "the Preparation" is known to have been a term for the day before the Sabbath, a day spent preparing for the Sabbath. Some have concluded that since there was a day known as "Preparation **of the Sabbath**" therefore there was a day before feasts known as "the Preparation **of the Passover**," and so forth. Based on that conclusion, they believe the passage under consideration says Jesus was tried by Pilate before the Passover (and therefore the supper of Jesus with His disciples before He was arrested could not have been the Passover).

But there are no indications in the Bible or other literature that the term "Preparation" was used in connection with feast days. It is known only to be a term for the sixth day of the week, or Friday. As used in John 19:14 it means "Friday of the Passover."

Gentiles named the days of the week after the planets and pagan gods—Sun's Day, Moon's Day, Tiw's Day, Woden's Day, Thor's Day, Frigg's Day and Saturn's Day. But the Jews named the days of the week simply the First Day, the Second Day, and so on. However, the special seventh day they named the Sabbath, and the special day before the Sabbath spent in preparation for the Sabbath they named the Preparation.

The Greek word for "Preparation" is *Paraskeue,* a word for Friday based on the Jewish usage, and still a word for Friday in modern Greek.[1]

Josephus used "the Preparation" as the name of the day before the Sabbath.[2]

The expression "the Preparation" appears in Matthew 27:62, Mark 15:42, Luke 23:54 and John 19:14,31, and 42. In all these passages it is either related to the Sabbath or it stands alone; none of these Bible passages show the term "Preparation" to refer to the day before a feast day. Mark clearly defines the term as referring to the day before the Sabbath: ". . . because it was the Preparation, that is, the day before the Sabbath" (Mk. 14:42)

The fact that "Preparation" in John 19:14 pertains directly to the Sabbath rather than to the first day of the feast is substantiated a bit later in the chapter when the day is simply called "the Preparation," and its significance is in its relationship to the Sabbath:

> *The Jews therefore, because it was the preparation, that the bodies should not remain upon the cross* **on** **the sabbath** *(for that sabbath day was an high day) besought Pilate that their legs might be broken, and that they might be taken away.* (Jn. 19:31)

The "sabbath" reference in John 19:31 is to "**the** Sabbath," which means only the seventh day. It is not a reference to "**a** sabbath," which might refer to a feast day. Feasts are like Sabbath days in certain respects; they are days of rest and consecration to the Lord. Sabbath, the word for the seventh day of rest, is the same as the Hebrew verb for "He rested" in Genesis 2:2,3 speaking of God resting on the seventh day. In Leviticus 23, the Sabbath seems to be called a feast (verses 2-3), and the expression "**a** sabbath" is used for three feasts: Trumpets (vs. 24-25), Day of Atonement (vs. 27-32), and Tabernacles (vs. 39-43). Each Sabbath is a feast; each feast is a day of rest and consecration to the Lord. But although a feast might be called "**a** sabbath," the terms "sabbath" and "feast" are not used interchangeably. A distinction between the two is made in verses 37-38. (Also in I Chron. 23:31; II Chron. 2:4; Lam. 2:6; Hos. 2:11; Col. 2:16 and the Mishnah[3]. If "sabbath" were another term for the feast day, John would not have said, "for that sabbath was a high day." Since all feasts were "high days", that would have been saying, "for that feast day was a feast day."

"The Passover" in John 19:14 refers to the entire eight-day feast. The Gospel writers and Josephus used "Passover" and "Feast of Unleavened Bread" interchangeably to refer to the eight days of the double feast thought of as one great feast.

The "Preparation of the Passover" was the Friday of the Passover feast. The "Sabbath of the Passover" was the Saturday that fell during the Passover feast. It was a special Sabbath—a "high day," or "great day" (Greek *megas*), because of having both the sacrifices and observances of the Sabbath and the sacrifices and observances of a day in the week of Unleavened Bread. Extra preparation was needed for such a Sabbath which fell on a feast day. Sometimes the Preparation of the Passover fell early during Passover week;

sometimes late, depending of course on the day of the week on which the 14th Nisan fell.

It is possible that "high day" in this verse refers to other ceremony and sacrifice in addition to that of the Sabbath and of one of the days of Unleavened Bread. It might also refer to the Day, or Feast, of Firstfruits.

The day for celebrating the Feast of Firstfruits which fell during the Week of Unleavened Bread has been disputed. The Sadducees interpreted "the morrow after the Sabbath" in Leviticus 23:11 as meaning the first day of the week (Sunday); they believed the Sunday of every Passover week was the proper day to observe the Day of Firstfruits with the wave ceremony and lamb sacrifice. Rabbis in later days interpreted "the Sabbath" in Leviticus 23:11 as another term for the First Day of Unleavened Bread, the 15th Nisan; therefore, they interpreted "morrow after the sabbath" to mean the 16th Nisan—which like the 14th and 15th would fall on different days of the week in different years. The Pharisees, from whom Rabbinical Judaism stems, apparently prevailed over the Sadducees in this matter in Jesus' day. Josephus says Firstfruits was observed on 16th Nisan.[4] The Sabbath of the Passover in the year Jesus was crucified, which was on the 16th Nisan, would also have been the Day of Firstfruits. The Sabbath would have been a "great day" not only because of extra sacrifices and observances of the Feast of Unleavened Bread, but also because of the extra wave ceremony and lamb sacrifice of the Feast of Firstfruits.

John 18:28—"it was early":

Then led they Jesus from Caiaphas unto the hall of judgment [to Pilate]: and it was early..."

It is important to understand what is meant by "early" in this reference to time during John's narrative of Jesus' trial before Pilate. Descriptions of this same time in the other

Gospels say:

> *When the morning was come, all the chief priests*
> *and elders of the people took counsel against Jesus to*
> *put him to death: And when they had bound him,*
> *they led him away, and delivered him to Pontius*
> *Pilate the governor.* (Matt. 27:1-2)

> *And straightway in the morning the chief priests*
> *held a consultation with the elders and scribes and*
> *the whole council, and bound Jesus, and carried*
> *him away, and delivered him to Pilate.* (Mk. 15:1)

> *And as soon as it was day, the elders of the people*
> *and the chief priests and the scribes came together,*
> *an led him into their council. . . And the whole*
> *multitude of them arose, and led him unto Pilate.*
> (Lk. 22:66-23:1)

These verses refer to morning of the next day, but to what time in the morning—an hour that would correspond to the modern 12:30 a.m., or to 9:00 a.m., or what?

The Greek word used for "early" and "morning" in John, Matthew, and Mark is *proios* which means "very early in the morning." The Greek word for "day" used by Luke is *hermera*, which can have as many meanings as the English word, including the technical midnight to midnight span called a day. Some words which the Gospel writers did **not** choose to describe the time of day under discussion are *auge* which means "brightness," "sunshine," "beginning of daylight," and "break of day," or the verb *orthros* which means "daybreak" and "early dawn," or the verb *epiphosko* which means "to dawn" or "to grow light" (the word used in Matt. 28:1).

The Gospel writers were communicating that it was technically the next morning (Friday), but it was the still-dark "wee hours" of the morning when the Jewish leaders took Jesus to Pilate. Such a use of *proios* is made in another place when Mark speaks of Jesus "in the morning" (*proi*) rising up "**a great while before day**" ("**while yet night**" according to the Greek) (Mk. 1:35). The word *hemera* which Luke used to describe the time Jesus was taken to Pilate is used in another place to speak of "night" hours: Jesus said to Peter, "this day (*hemera*), **even in this night**, before the cock crow twice, thou shalt deny me thrice." (Mk. 14:30). It was, in fact, right after this cock crowing in the night that Jesus was led to Pilate (cf Mark 14:72-15:1).

Jesus was arrested after His Passover meal and after His hour or so of prayer in the Garden. (Possibly about 11:00 p.m. to 1:00 a.m.?) He spent some amount of time over an hour in the palace of the High Priest being questioned by Caiaphas and the other Jewish leaders (see Luke 22:59-61), and then was taken to Pilate when it was "early" (2:00-3:00 a.m. or so?).

While Jesus was being interrogated by the religious leaders, the multitude who had arrested Him lit a fire for warmth in the courtyard of the High Priest's palace (Mk. 14:54; Lk. 22:55; Jn. 18:25). This fire was for warmth because it was cold in the middle of the night in springtime Palestine.

In New Testament times there were four "watches of the night." (See Mk. 13:35). The "cockcrow watch" was before the "morning watch," and began around 2:30 a.m. Based on Jesus' statement about the cock crowing in the night, and the naming and timing of the "cockcrow watch," cocks did crow in Jerusalem during the "wee hours" of the morning. A twelve-year observation verifies this.[5]

Undoubtedly Roman officials, as well as the Jewish multitudes, were awake in Jerusalem on Passover night when the city was alive with the celebration of the Feast. It is not unexpected that Pilate should be awake to receive the Jewish leaders in the middle of that night. Even apart from Passover, some Roman rulers were known to begin and complete their work day very early. The emperor Vespasian began his work day before dawn. Pliny the Elder had completed his work day by the fourth or fifth hour.[6] Plutarch, Pliny and other Romans calculated the civil day from midnight to midnight.[7]

John 18:28—"eat the passover":

Then led they Jesus from Caiaphas unto the hall of judgment: and it was early; and they themselves went not into the judgment hall, lest they should be defiled; but that they might eat the passover. Pilate then went out unto them. . .

The eating of the passover is yet future **for the religious leaders** in this passage. (Others have already eaten it.) This passage indicates that entering a Gentile building was a defilement to a Jew according to laws of the day. The religious leaders could not eat the passover if they were ritually unclean by the defilement of entering the Gentile judgment hall.

The Law said such a defilement lasted until sunset (Lev. 15:5f. See also the Apocryphal book of Judith, 12:8-10.) The religious leaders have a defilement problem because it is Friday morning of the 15th Nisan in the very early hours and they have only a few hours left until the sunrise deadline which the Law set for eating the passover. They have not yet eaten it in their busyness of arresting and trying Jesus following Judas's betrayal. The sunrise deadline would come before the sunset that would make them clean.

Those who interpret "Preparation" of John 19 as the day before the Feast (Thursday), rather than Friday, and who interpret "early" and "morning" as 6:00 a.m. or so on the day the passover lambs were sacrificed, have a problem with this verse. If John 18:28 were Thursday morning of the day the lambs were sacrificed, the Jewish leaders would not have been concerned about defilement from entering the judgment hall because such defilement would end at sunset and they would be able to eat the passover that night. The expression, "**eat** the passover" is an evidence that this incident could not have been the morning of the 14th. If it were the morning of the 14th, the Jewish leaders would have been concerned about defilement keeping them from **sacrificing** the passover.

Some say the view that John 18:28 speaks of Friday morning (15th Nisan) in the wee hours could not be correct because the passover had to be eaten by midnight, according to the Mishnah, and it was after midnight here (because it was the morning of the next day.) This protest is groundless, first because the Mishnah midnight rule did not pertain to Jesus' day, and second, because even if it did, the Mishnah agrees with the Law that the true deadline for eating the passover is dawn.

The Law decreed that the passover lamb had to be eaten in the night of the 15th Nisan before morning of the 15th (the morning of the 15th coming after the evening of the 15th, by Hebrew reckoning) (Ex. 12:10; Nu. 9:12; Deut. 16:4). The Hebrew word for the morning deadline is *boker*. The meaning is a specific point at which night turns into morning—namely sunrise or daybreak.

While the Law allowed until sunrise to eat the passover lamb, Jewish religious leaders traditionally set the dealine much earlier to keep everybody from getting close to the deadline and transgressing it. In the time of the book of Jubilees, the traditional deadline was 2:00 a.m. By Philo's time (Jesus' day), that deadline had veen waived due to the huge number of pilgrims in Jerusalem sacrificing lambs in shifts and eating them as possible thereafter. But the Law of Moses —the sunrise deadline—was still binding.

The later Mishnah, representing the tradition of Jews in the Diaspora celebrating Passover without a Temple and passover sacrifice, set midnight as the deadline for completing the Seder and eating the ritual foods.[8] Passover was no longer observed in Jerusalem; there were no pilgrim crowds and thousands of animal sacrifices causing a time squeeze. Midnight was as late a dealine as anyone normally needed to prepare a Seder plate and eat its foods. Yet the Rabbis who wrote the Mishnah— who did not presume to override the Law—stretched the deadline from midnight to sunrise for necessary exceptions. They explained that sunrise was the true deadline, and tell why they set midnight:

> Moreover, wheresoever the sages prescribe "until midnight" the duty of fulfillment lasts until the rise of dawn... Why then have the sages said: Until midnight? To keep a man far from transgression.[9]

John 19:14—"the sixth hour":

> And it was the preparation of the passover, and about the sixth hour: and he saith unto the Jews, Behold your King!

In order to harmonize John's chronology with the other Gospels, it is necessary to define how John calculated time and what he meant by "the sixth hour" in the 19:15 reference.

When interpreting references to dates and times in the New Testament it must be remembered that the Jews and Romans calculated dates differently. For the Jews, a new day technically began at sunset; for the Romans, at midnight. (see chart at the end of this appendix illustrating Jewish-Roman days overlap.)

Time could not be figured precisely in those days when there were no clocks, and the average person did not have routine access to a sundial. References to time were approximated. As in modern times, there was the technical day figured from midnight to midnight (by the Roman method), or from sunset to sunset (by the Jewish method). But there was also the "practical" day—the hours of daylight in which most work was done. Jesus' question, "Are there not twelve hours in the day?" (Jn. 11:9) has to do with the approximate amount of daylight in which work might be done. The night was divided into four watches in New Testament times under Roman influence.

There were different methods of calculating the hour of the day. Some began counting the hours of the day from 6:00 a.m., the practical beginning of the day. Others estimated the hours of the day from 12:00 midnight, the Roman technical beginning of the day. By the latter method, the hours of the afternoon-evening were calculated from noon onwards (as in modern times with clocks). Without the addition of "a.m." or "p.m." to a designated hour, the context determined whether it was morning or evening.

The Synoptic Gospel writers calculated the time of day from 6:00 a.m. Thus Friday's third hour when Jesus was crucified (Mk. 15:25) was 9:00 a.m. The sixth to ninth hours when darkness came (Mk. 15:33; Lk. 23:44) was 12:00 noon to 3:00 p.m. Jesus gave up His spirit right after that. Josephus also calculated time in this manner in reference to Temple-time practice. He said the passover lambs were slain from the ninth to the eleventh hour, or from 3:00 to 5:00 p.m.[10]

John, however, wrote his Gospel much later than Matthew, Mark and Luke. The Temple which still stood when the synoptic Gospels were written had been gone about twenty years when John wrote. No longer did a trumpet blast from the Temple signal the beginning and ending of the Jewish sabbath day.[11] John's readers included many more Gentiles than the Synoptics' readers, and they would be most familiar with the Roman method of reckoning days and time.

John wrote of a day's span in the Roman way—a morning followed by the evening, not in the Jewish way—an evening followed by the morning. In chapter 20, for example, he wrote of Mary Magdalene coming to the tomb very early in the morning of the first day of the week (vs. 1) and followed that with an account which says, "when therefore it was evening, **on that day,** the first day of the week..." (vs. 19).

John wrote of hours in the Roman technical way, calculating

from midnight or from noon. All of John's many references to time and hours were by this method of calculation. The woman at the well (Jn. 4:11), for example, came to draw water at the sixth hour, 6:00 p.m.—the customary evening time when women drew water. The "sixth hour" of John 19:14, according to its context, was 6:00 a.m.

Jesus had been brought before Pilate in the early morning hours according to a harmony of all the Gospels. There is a time lapse of an indefinite period between John 19:12 and the "sixth hour" reference in 19:14: "And **from thenceforth** Pilate sought to release him." Perhaps it is during this indefinite period of time that Pilate sent Jesus to Herod— a matter reported only by Luke (23:6-13). Luke says Herod sent Jesus back to Pilate and after that Pilate **reconvened** the Jewish religious leaders (who had gone home or to the Temple to eat the passover?) Then at the sixth hour, 6:00 a.m. Friday, Pilate said to the Jews, "Behold your King!"

Some Other Passover References

There are a few other Passover-related references in the Gospels which are sometimes cited as proof that the Last Supper (in all four Gospels) could not have been the Passover because the references supposedly contradict the Law and/or the Mishnah.

Supposed Omissions: Some say the Last Supper could not have been a Passover meal because the Gospel accounts do not mention the passover lamb or the Exodus story retelling— essential elements of Passover observance. The simple answer to this is that the Gospels do not indicate that these elements were absent. Rather, the references to Jesus' disciples preparing for and eating the passover, which they celebrated as did all the nation, implies getting a lamb and sacrificing it, and retelling the Exodus events as required. It was not the Gospel writers' purpose to repeat what the Law said about the passover lamb or the Exodus event; it was their purpose to move into the New Covenant teaching of the Lamb of God Who fulfilled these things. In all the Mishnah, which moves from the Law to the new Rabbinical Judaism Passover observance, there is only one slight reference to the passover lamb even though the Mishnah Passover tractate is named *"Pesachim"* (passover lambs.)

Family Festival: Since Passover is a family festival, some say the Last Supper which Jesus ate with His disciples could not have been the Passover meal. The Last Supper more resembles a *kiddush*, a fellowship meal, they say. In regard to this, it is incorrect to assume that only the Twelve Apostles were present at the Last Supper. The Gospel accounts allow for, and in fact seem to call for, the interpretation that all of Jesus' disciples (including believing families) were present for the upper room Last Supper. (see page 48.)

Working: Certain references in the Gospels about "work" during Passover are sometimes cited as being in contradiction to the Law and/or the Mishnah. The critics who cite these work "facts" consider them evidence that the Last Supper was not the Passover.

It is said that it was considered "work," and therefore illegal, to carry swords or other weapons on a feast day, as did Peter and the multitude who arrested Jesus (Matt. 26:47, 51; Mk. 14:43, 47; Lk. 22:49-50; Jn. 18:3, 10). This is supposed to be evidence that Jesus was not arrested on the eve of the Feast of Unleavened Bread. But there is nothing in the Law against carrying weapons on the Passover feast day. The Law says only that no **servile** work could be done—no regular menial work (Ex. 12:16; Lev. 23:7, 8; Nu. 28:18). Laws for the Sabbath were stricter than for feasts. The Mishnah commentary does not speak to the matter of weapons on a feast day, but on the Sabbath. And the Mishnah rabbis give different viewpoints about going out with weapons on the Sabbath. One viewpoint is that the man who does go out on the Sabbath carrying a weapon is liable for a sin offering. Another is that a man may go out with swords and other weapons on the Sabbath because they are his adornments.[12]

Kindling a fire is said to have been illegal on Passover. The multitude who arrested Jesus could not have done so on the eve of the Feast, it is concluded, because they kindled a fire (Mk. 14:54; Lk. 22:55; Jn. 18:18). This assumption is incorrect. If in fact later Mishnah tradition about Sabbath fire kindling also applied to feasts, it still would not have pertained to Jesus' day. The Law did not make it illegal to kindle a fire on Passover. The Law says only that it is illegal on the Sabbath (Ex. 35:3). In fact fires had to be kindled to roast the passover lambs in Temple days.

It has been asserted that Simon the Cyrene who carried Jesus' cross had been "working in the fields" because he was "coming in from the fields." (Therefore, the day Jesus was crucified was not a feast day because it was a work day.) This argument is built upon interpreting *agron* in Mark 15:21 and Luke 23:26 as "field" and upon the assumption that Simon must have been working if he had been "in the field." *Agron* is normally translated "farm" or "country." Even if Simon had been a native of the area living on a farm outside the city, he would not have been coming into Jerusalem at 8:00-8:30 a.m. from a day's work on his farm. The designation "Cyrene" tells the reader that Simon was not in fact a native. He was from Cyrene in Libya of North Africa. He was undoubltedly a Passover pilgrim lodging outside the city of Jersualem, as many did during the Feast, coming into Jerusalem from the surrounding country every morning of the Feast.

It is said that Nicodemus and the women who prepared spices, and Joseph of Arimathea who purchased a burial cloth, for Jesus' body would all have been engaged in "illegal" Jewish customs if the New Testament Passover chronology were correct. (See Matt. 27:59; Mk. 15:46; Lk. 23:53; Jn. 19:40.) But there is nothing in the Law against these activities as they occurred during the feast and as reported by the Gospel writers. Jesus' disciples are depicted in the Gospels as complying with Sabbath laws concerning burial. It was before the beginning of the Sabbath that Joseph of Arimathea bought the burial cloth (Lk. 23:53-54) and the woman prepared the burial spices (Lk. 23:56). Nicodemus applied his spices to Jesus' body before the Sabbath (Jn. 19:39-42). The women waited until the Sabbath was over to bring their spices to the tomb (Mk. 16:1; Lk. 23:56-24:1). The Mishnah, for comparison, says, "They may await nightfall at the Sabbath limit to see to the business of [the reception of] a bride or of [the burial of] a corpse, to fetch its coffin and wrappings."[13] Also, "They may make ready [on the Sabbath] all that is needful for the dead, and anoint it and wash it, provided that they do not move any member of it."[14]

Purchasing Passover Food or Giving Alms: In the account of Judas leaving the Passover meal in John 13:29 it is said that some of the disciples thought, because Judas had the money bag, Jesus had told him to buy something needed for the feast or to give alms to the poor. Some say this argues against the Last Supper being the Passover because no one would leave the feast to buy for the feast, and because if it were Pasover all the poor would be in homes somewhere drinking the four cups of wine the Mishnah says even the poor must drink on Passover.

The New Testament account is not in contradiction to either the Law or the Mishnah in describing a situation where one might leave the feast to buy for the feast. The Law (Ex. 12:16) and the Mishnah[15] both state that it was legal to do what was necessary to prepare for the Passover meal on the first day of the festival. Beyond that, it must be pointed out again that the Mishnah describes a later, more formal, and different meal tradition than that described in the New Testament.

It does not follow that the Mishnah declaration about the poor drinking four cups of wine on Passover is an evidence that all the poor were cared for on Passover. Even if this were so in the Mishnah's post-Temple days, it was not necessarily so in Jesus' day, and apparently it was not. The Apostles who were present at the meal with Jesus wrote of that which was possible in their day. The secondary Mishnah document is not a greater authority on Passover in Jesus' day than the primary New Testament documents.

Trial on a Feast Day: Much has been written about the illegality of a Jewish trial on a feast day because of the Mishnah statement, "Therefore trials may not be held on the eve of a Sabbath or on the eve of a festival day."[16] The trial of Jesus on the eve of the Feast of Unleavened Bread is pointed out to be an example of Gosepl error.

If the Gospels' chronology that Jesus was tried in the night of the 15th Nisan is wrong, as some maintain, then He was tried on the 14th Nisan—also a feast day.

The Mishnah and the New Testament may or may not be in contradiction on this matter. It may be that the Mishnah trial law is later and does not pertain to the New Testament period. It is also possible that the *Sanhedrin* who tried Jesus was not the same body of religious leaders as the *Beth Din* associated with Mishnah commentary.[17]

The Law of Moses required the punishment for certain offenses to be published in such a way that all the people of the entire nation, would "hear and fear and do no more presumptuously" (Deut. 17:13 and 21:21). This was interpreted in early Jewish commentary as meaning execution should take place during one of the three pilgrim feasts—the only times **all** the people were gathered.[18]

The New Testament writers record that the Jewish leaders planned to take Jesus and kill Him, but not on the feast day. Their concern for avoiding the feast day had not to do with any law, but with avoiding a riot (Matt. 26:3-5; Mk. 14:1-2). They tried to kill Jesus by stoning on the Feast of Dedication (Jn. 10:22,31). They tried to arrest Him in "the great day" of the Feast of Tabernacles (Jn. 7:2, 37, 44-45).

Footnotes:

[1] A.T. Robertson, *A Harmony of the Gospels* (New York: Harper and Bros. Publishers, 1922), p. 282.

[2] Josephus, *Antiquities*, xvi, vi, ii.

[3] *Mishnah*, Sanhedrin 4:1.

[4] Josephus, *Antiquities*, iii, x, v.

[5] William L. Lane, *Commentary on the Gospel of Mark* (Wm. B. Eerdmans, 1974), p. 543

[6] A.N. Sherwin-White, *Roman Society and Roman Law in the New Testament* (Grand Rapids, Mich., 1963), pp. 45-46.

[7] A.T. Robertson, *op. cit.*, p. 286.

[8] *Mishnah*, Pesachim 10:9.

[9] *Mishnah*, Berakoth 1:1

[10] Josephus, *Wars*, vi, ix, iii.

[11] Josephus, *Wars*, iv, ix, xii.

[12] *Mishnah*, Shabbath 6:4

[13] *Mishnah*, Shabbath 23:4

[14] *Mishnah*, Shabbath 23:5.

[15] *Mishnah*, Pesachim 6:2.

[16] *Mishnah*, Sanhedrin 4:1. See also Sanhedrin 5:5.

[17] Ellis Rivkin, "Beth Din, Boule, Sanhedrin: A Tragedy of Errors," *Hebrew Union College Annual*, Vol. 46 (1975), pp. 181-199.

[18] *Tosefta*, Sanhedrin 11:7. Also Joh Ylvisaker, *The Gospels* (Minneapolis, Minn.: Augsburg Publishing House, 1932), p. 640. Also William L. Lane, *op. cit.*, p. 497.

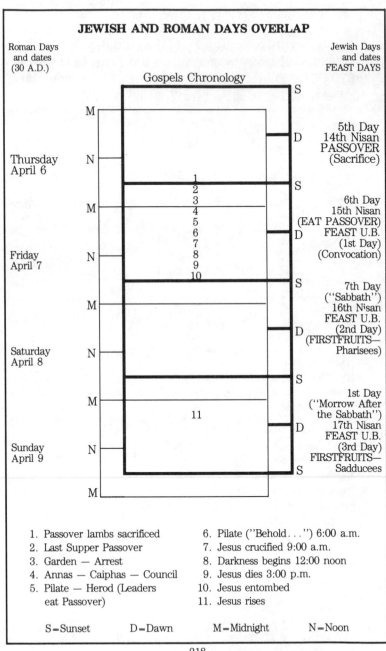

JEWISH AND ROMAN DAYS OVERLAP

Roman Days
and dates
(30 A.D.)

Jewish Days
and dates
FEAST DAYS

Gospels Chronology

S

M

D
5th Day
14th Nisan
PASSOVER
(Sacrifice)

Thursday
April 6
N

1
2
S

3
M
6th Day
15th Nisan
(EAT PASSOVER)
FEAST U.B.
(1st Day)
(Convocation)

4
5
6
7
D

Friday
April 7
N
8
9
10

S
7th Day
("Sabbath")
16th Nisan
FEAST U.B.
(2nd Day)
(FIRSTFRUITS—
Pharisees)

M

D

Saturday
April 8
N

S
1st Day
("Morrow After
the Sabbath")
17th Nisan
FEAST U.B.
(3rd Day)
FIRSTFRUITS—
Sadducees

M
11

D

Sunday
April 9
N

S

M

1. Passover lambs sacrificed
2. Last Supper Passover
3. Garden — Arrest
4. Annas — Caiphas — Council
5. Pilate — Herod (Leaders
   eat Passover)

6. Pilate ("Behold...") 6:00 a.m.
7. Jesus crucified 9:00 a.m.
8. Darkness begins 12:00 noon
9. Jesus dies 3:00 p.m.
10. Jesus entombed
11. Jesus rises

S = Sunset   D = Dawn   M = Midnight   N = Noon

218

BIBLIOGRAPHY

This complete listing of sources consulted is provided for the benefit of students. A few of the less-technical and more-accessible titles are indicated by asterisks; these books recommended for laymen are categorized at the end of the Bibliography.

BOOKS

Bagatti, Bellarmino. *The Church From the Circumcision: History and Archaeology of the Judeo-Christians.* Trans. by Eugene Hoade. Jerusalem: Franciscan Press, 1971.

―――― *The Church From the Gentiles in Palestine: History and Archaeology.* Trans. by Eugene Hoade. Jerusalem: Franciscan Press, 1971.

Barclay, William. *The Gospel of John.* Vol. 2. Philadelphia: The Westminster Press, 1955.

Bokser, Baruch M. *The Origins of the Seder.* Los Angeles: University of California Press, 1984.

Broadus, John A. *A Harmony of the Gospels.* New York: A.C. Armstrong & Son, 1895.

Bronstein, David. *The Jewish Passover and the Christian Communion.* Chicago: Rev. David Bronstein, 1941.

Brown, Raymond E. *The Gospel According to John.* Vol. 1. New York: Garden City, c1966.

Cairns, Earle E. *Christianity Through the Centuries: A History of the Christian Church.* Grand Rapids, Mich.: Zondervan Publishing House, 1954, revised 1967.

Carrington, Philip. *The Early Christian Church.* Vol. 1. *The First Christian Century.* Cambridge: University Press, 1957.

Coulter, Frederick R. *A Harmony of the Gospels in Modern English.* Los Angeles: York Publishing Co., 1974.

Danielou, Jean and Marrou Henri. *The Christian Centuries: A New History of the Catholic Church.* Vol. 1. *The First 600 Years.* New York: McGraw-Hill Book Company, 1964.

Daube, David. *The New Testament and Rabbinic Judaism.* London: University of London, The Athlone Press, 1956.

Davies, J.G. *The Early Christian Church.* New York: Holt, Rinehart & Winston, 1965.

Davies, W.D. *Christian Origins and Judaism.* Philadelphia: The Westminster Press, 1962.

Dix, Dom Gregory. *Jew and Greek. A Study in the Primitive Church.* Westminster: Dacre Press, 1953.

*Donin, Hayim Halevy. *To Be A Jew.* New York: Basic Books, Inc. Publishers, 1972.

Duchesne, Louis. *Early History of the Christian Church.* Vol. 1. *From Its Foundation to the End of the Fifth Century.* London: John Murray, 1909.

Early Christian Fathers. Ed. by Cyril C. Richardson. New York: Macmillan Publishing Co., Inc., 1970.

Eban, Abba. *Heritage: Civilization and the Jews.* New York: Summit Books, 1984.

*Eckstein, Yechiel. *What Christians Should Know About Jews and Judaism.* Waco, Texas: Word Books, 1984.

Edersheim, Alfred. *The History of the Jewish Nation After the Destruction of Jerusalem Under Titus.* Grand Rapids, Mich.: Baker Book House, 1895 publication republished in paperback, 1979.

_____ *The Life and Times of Jesus the Messiah.* Vol. II. New York: Longmans, Green & Co., 1899.

_____ *The Temple: Its Ministry and Services As They Were at the Time of Jesus Christ.* Grand Rapids, Mich.: Wm. B. Eerdmans Publ. Co., n.d. Reprinted 1958.

*Eusebius Pamphilus. *Ecclesiastical History.* Grand Rapids, Mich.: Baker Book House, 1955.

*Eusebius. *The History of the Church From Christ to Constantine.* Trans. by G.A. Williams. Baltimore, MD.; Penguin Books, 1965.

Feeley-Harnik, Gillian, *The Lord's Table: Eucharist and Passover in Early Christianity.* Philadelphia: University of Pennsylvania Press, 1981.

Finegan, Jack. *Light From the Ancient Past.* Princeton, N.J.: Princeton University Press, 1946.

Fisher, George Park. *History of the Christian Church.* New York: Charles Schribner's Sons, 1923.

Foakes-Jackson, F.J. *The Rise of Gentile Christianity.* New York: George H. Doran Co., 1927.

Frend, W.H.C. *The Early Church.* Philadelphia: J.B. Lippincott Company, 1966.

Fruchtenbaum, Arnold G. *Hebrew Christianity: Its Theology, History and Philosophy.* Washington, D.C.: Canon Press, 1974.

*Gade, Richard E. *A Historical Survey of Anti-Semitism.* Grand Rapids, Mich.: Baker Book House, 1981.

Gaster, Theodor Herzl. *Passover: Its History and Traditions.* New York: Henry Schuman, 1949.

Glover, T.R. *The Conflict of Religions in the Early Roman Empire.* London: Methuen & Co., Ltd., 1909.

Goble, Philip E. *Everything You Need to Grow a Messianic Synagogue.* South Pasadena, Ca.: William Carey Library, 1974.

Goguel, Maurice. *The Birth of Christianity.* Trans. by H.C. Snape. New York: The MacMillan Company, 1954.

*Goldberg, Louis. *Our Jewish Friends.* Chicago: Moody Press, 1977.

*Goodman, Philip. *The Passover Anthology.* Philadelphia: The Jewish Publication Society of America, 1961.

Goppelt, Leonhard. *Apostolic and Post-Apostolic Times.* Trans. by Robert A. Guelich. New York: Harper & Row, Publishers, 1970

Gray, George Buchanan. *Sacrifice in the Old Testament: Its Theology and Practice.* New York: KTAV Publishing House, 1971.

Greenslade, S.L. *Schism in the Early Church.* London: SCM Press, Ltd., 1953.

Guilding, Aileen. *The Fourth Gospel and Jewish Worship.* Oxford: Clarendon Press, 1960.

**Haggadah Shel Pesach.* Complimentary Edition of the Traditional Haggadah Passover Seder Service. Published by Maxwell House. No Date.

Hole, Christina. *Easter and Its Customs.* New York: M. Barrows and Co., Inc., 1961.

Hunt, B.P.W. Stather. *Some Johannine Problems.* London: Skiffington & Son, Ltd., 1958.

Josephus, Flavius. *Josephus: Complete Works.* Trans. by William Whiston. Grand Rapids, Mich.: Kregel Publications, 1960.

Justin Martyr. *The Dialogue With Trypho.* Trans., Introduction and Notes by A. Lukyn Williams. New York: The Macmillan Co., 1930.

Kertzer, Morris N. *What Is A Jew?* New York: Collier Books: A Division of Macmillan Publishing Co., Inc., 1978.

Klijn, A.F.J. and Reinink, G.J. *Patristic Evidence For Jewish-Christian Sects.* Leiden: E.J. Brill, 1973.

Lane, William L. *Commentary on the Gospel of Mark.* Grand Rapids, Mich., Wm. B. Eerdmans, 1974.

Latourette, Kenneth Scott. *A History of the Expansion of Christianity.* Vol.I: *The First Five Centuries.* New York: Harper & Brothers Publishers, 1937.

Lechler, Gotthard Victor. *The Apostolic and Post Apostolic Times.* Edinburg: T & T Clark, 1886.

Levy, Isaac. *A Guide to Passover.* London: Jewish Chronicle Publications, 1958.

Lightfoot, John. *Horae Hebraicae et Talmudicae: Hebrew & Talmudic Exercitations Upon the Gospels, Acts, Some Chapters of Romans and I Corinthians.* A New Edition by Rev. R. Gandell. 4 Vols. London: Oxford University Press, 1859.

Lightfoot, Robert Henry. *History and Interpretation in the Gospels.* New York: Harper & Bros. Publishers, 1934.

*Lipson, Eric-Peter. *Passover Haggadah.* San Francisco: JFJ Publishing, 1986.

*Lord, Priscilla Sawyer and Foley, Daniel J. *Easter Garland.* Philadelphia: Chilton Company, 1963.

MacDonald, Alexander B. *Christian Worship in the Primitive Church.* Edinburg: T & T Clark, 1934.

Maxwell, William D. *An Outline of Christian Worship.* London: Oxford University Press, 1936.

Mishnah. Trans. by Herbert Danby. London: Oxford University Press, 1933.

Neander, Augustus. *History of the Planting and Training of the Christian Church by the Apostles.* Trans. by J.E. Ryland. New York: Sheldon & Company, 1869.

Newman, Louis Israel. *Jewish Influence on Christian Reform Movements.* New York: Columbia University Press, 1925.

Oesterley, W O E. *The Jewish Background of the Christian Liturgy.* Gloucester, Mass.: Peter Smith, 1965. (First Printed by Oxford University Press, 1925.)

Pfleiderer, Otto. *Christian Origins.* Trans. by Daniel A. Huebsch. London: T. Fisher Unwin, 1906.

Potok, Chaim. *Wanderings: Chaim Potok's History of the Jews.* New York: Fawcett Crest, 1978.

Qualben, Lars P. *A History of the Christian Church.* New York: Thos. Nelson & Sons, 1933.

*Raphael, Chaim. *A Feast of History: Passover Through the Ages as a Key to Jewish Experience (With a New Translation of the Haggadah For Use at the Seder.)* New York: Simon & Schuster, 1972.

Rausch, David A. *Messianic Judaism: Its History, Theology, and Polity.* Texts and Studies in Religion. Vol. 14. N.Y. & Toronto: The Edwin Mellen Press, 1982.

Reumann, John. *The Supper of the Lord*. Philadelphia: Fortress Press, 1985.

Robinson, Edward. *A Harmony of the Four Gospels in English*. Boston: Houghton Mifflin Co., 1846.

Robertson, A.T. *A Harmony of the Gospels*. New York: Harper & Bros. Publishers, 1922.

*Rosen, Ceil and Moishe. *Christ in the Passover*. Chicago: Moody Press, 1978.

Rosen, Moishe with Proctor, William. *Jews For Jesus*. Old Tappan, N.J.: Fleming H. Revell Co., 1974.

Sanday, William, *The Criticism of the Fourth Gospel*. New York: Chas. Scribner's Sons, 1905.

Sandmel, Samuel. *Judaism and Christian Beginnings*. New York: Oxford University Press, 1978.

_____ *The First Christian Century in Judaism and Christianity: Certainties and Uncertainties*. New York: Oxford University Press, 1969.

Schaff, Philip. *History of the Christian Church*. Vol. I & II. New York: Scribner, Armstrong & Co., 1873.

Schauss, Hayyim. *The Jewish Festivals*. Trans. by Samuel Jaffee. Cincinnati: Union of American Hebrew Congregations, 1938.

Scott, James Julius Jr. *The Church of Jerusalem A.D. 30-100: An Investigation of the Growth of Internal Factions and the Extension of Its Influence in the Larger Church*. A Thesis Presented to the University of Manchester In Application For the Degree of Doctor of Philosophy. Oct. 1969. (University Microfilms International, Ann Arbor, Mich., 1982)

Sechrist, Elizabeth Hough and Woolsey, Janette. *It's Time For Easter*. Philadelphia: Macrae Smith Co., 1961.

Segal, J. B. *The Hebrew Passover From the Earliest Times to A.D. 70*. London: Oxford University Press, 1963.

Shelley, Bruce. *Church History in Plain Language*. Waco, Texas: Word Books, 1982.

Sherwin-White, A.N. *Roman Society and Roman Law in the New Testament*. Grand Rapids, Mich.: Baker Book House, 1963.

Smith, M.A. *From Christ to Constantine*. Downers Grove, Ill.: Inter-Varisity Press, 1971.

Sobel, B.Z. *Hebrew Christianity: The Thirteenth Tribe*. New York: John Wiley & Sons, 1974.

Stevens, William Arnold and Burton, Ernest De Witt. *A Harmony of the Gospels For Historical Study*. New York: Chas. Scribner's Sons, 1932.

Strack, Hermann L. *Introduction to the Talmud and Midrash*. Philadelphia: Jewish Publication Society of America, 1931.

Strong, James. *The Exhaustive Concordance of the the Bible*. New York: Abingdon Press, 1890.

Swanson, Reuben J. *The Horizontal Line Synopsis of the Gospels*. Dillsboro, N. Carolina: Western North Carolina Press, Inc., 1975.

The Apostolic Fathers. Ed. and Trans. by J.B. Lightfoot. Two Parts in Five Volumes. Grand Rapids, Mich.: Baker Book House, Printed in 1981.

The Babylonian Talmud. 35 Vol. Trans. by Rabbi Isidore Epstein. London: the Soncino Press, 1930s.

The Babylonian Talmud. 20 Vols in 10. Trans. by Michael L. Rodkinson. Boston: the Talmud Society, 1918.

The Cambridge Medieval History. Vol. I: *The Christian Roman Empire.* Ed. by H.M. Gwatkin and J.P. Whitney. London: Cambridge University Press, 1911.

The Synoptic Gospels. C.G. Montefiore, ed. Vol. II. New York: KTAV Publishing House, Inc., 1968.

Tenney, Merrill C. *John: The Gospel of Belief. An Analytic Study of the Text.* Grand Rapids, Mich.: Wm. B. Eerdmans Publishing Co., 1948.

The Tripe of the Samaritans Priests in Nablus. *The Celebration of Passover By the Samaritans.* Jerusalem: Greek Convent Press, n.d.

Tuchman, Barbara W. *Bible and Sword: England and Palestine From the Bronze Age to Balfour.* New York: Ballantine Books, A Division of Random House, Inc., 1956 & 1984.

Tyson, Joseph B. *A Study of Early Christianity.* New York: The Macmillan Co., 1973.

Walker, Williston. *A History of the Christian Church.* New York: Charles Scribner's Sons, 1959.

*Watts, Alan W. *Easter: Its Story and Meaning.* New York: Henry Schuman, 1950.

Weiser, Francis X. *Handbook of Christian Feasts and Customs.* New York: Harcourt, Brace & Co., 1952.

* _____ *The Easter Book.* New York: Harcourt, Brace & Co., 1954.

Wieland, Albert Cassel. *A New Harmony of the Gospels.* Grand Rapids, Mich.: Wm. B. Eerdmans Publ. Co., 1947.

Williams, Robert R. *A Guide to the Teachings of the Early Church Fathers.* Grand Rapids, Mich.: Wm. B. Eerdmans Publ. Co., 1960.

Woodbridge, John D. and Noll, Mark A. and Hatch, Nathan O. *The Gospel in America: Themes in the Story of America's Evangelicals.* Grand Rapids, Mich.: Zondervan Publishing House, 1979.

Ylvisaker, Joh. *The Gospels.* Minneapolis, Minn.: Augsburg Publishing House, 1932.

ARTICLES

Barton, George A. "On the Trial of Jesus Before the Sanhedrin," *Journal of Biblical Literature,* Vol. 41 (1922), 205-211.

_____ "The Origin of the Discrepancy Between the Synoptists and the Fourth Gospel As to the Date and Character of Christ's Last Supper With His Disciples," *Journal of Biblical Literature,* Vol. 43 (1924), 28-31.

Baumgarten, Joseph M. "The Beginning of the Day in the Calendar of Jubilees," *Journal of Biblical Literature,* Vol. 77 (1958), 355-360.

Buse, Ivor. "St. John and the Passion Narratives of St. Matthew and St. Luke," *New Testament Studies,* Vol. 7 (1960), 65-76.

Danby, H. "The Bearing of the Rabbinical Criminal Code on the Jewish Trial Narratives in the Gospels," *Journal of Theological Studies* Vol. 21 (1920), 51-76.

Flight, John W. "The Nomadic Idea and Ideal in the Old Testament (Section on Feasts and Holy Seasons)," *Journal of Biblical Literature*, Vol. 42 (1923), 206-209 (Section consulted)

Gray, E.P. "The Last Passover and Its Harmonies," *Bibliotheca Sacra*, Vol. 51 (1894), 339-346.

Jeremias, Joachim. "The Last Supper," *Journal of Theological Studies*, (Old Series) Vol. 50 (1949), 1-10.

———— "Review of Annie Jaubert's book: *La Date de la Cene: Calendrier biblique et liturgie chritienne,"* *Journal of Theological Studies*, Vol. 10 (1959) 131-133.

May, H.G. "Relation of Passover to the Festival of Unleavened Cakes," *Journal of Biblical Studies*, Vol. 55 (1936), 65-82.

Monks, George Gardner. "The Lucan Account of the Last Supper," *Journal of Biblical Studies*, Vol. 44 (1925), 228-260.

Moulton, Warren J. "The Samaritans Passover," *Journal of Biblical Literature*, Vol. 22 (1903), 187-194.

Petuchowski, Jakob J. "This Do In Remembrance of Me," *Journal of Biblical Literature*, Vol. 76 (1957), 293-298.

Rivkin, Ellis. "Beth Din, Boule, Sanhedrin: A Tragedy of Errors," *Hebrew Union College Annual*, Vol. 46 (1977), 181-199.

Robinson, E. "The Alleged Discrepancy Between John and the Other Evangelists Respecting Our Lord's Last Passover,"*Bibliotheca Sacra*, Vol. 2 (1845), 405-436.

Schmidt, Nathaniel. "The Character of Christ's Last Meal," *Journal of Biblical Literature*, Vol. 11 (1892), 1-21.

Temple, Sydney. "The Two Traditions of the Last Supper, Betrayal and Arrest," *New Testament Studies*, Vol. 7 (1960), 77-85.

Torrey, Charles C. "The Date of the Crucifixion According to the Fourth Gospel," *Journal of Biblical Literature*, Vol. 50 (1931), 227-241.

Walther, James A. "The Chronology of Passion Week," *Journal of Biblical Literature*, Vol. 77 (1958), 116-122.

Zeitlin, Solomon. "The Beginning of the Day in the Calendar of Jubilees," *Journal of Biblical Literature*, Vol. 78 (1959), 153-156.

———— "The Date of the Crucifixion According to the Fourth Gospel," *Journal of Biblical Literature*, Vol. 51 (1932), 263-271.

*RECOMMENDED READING

HISTORY OF PASSOVER AND THE HAGGADAH

Goodman, Philip. *The Passover Anthology.* (Includes Primary Documents.)

Raphael, Chaim. *A Feast of History.* (Includes a new translation of the Haggadah.)

EARLY CHURCH HISTORY

Eusebius, Pamphilus. *Ecclesiastical History.* (Appendices include the canons of the Council of Nicea and complete text of Constantine's letter to the churches after the Council. Eusebius had a pro-Constantine, anti-Quartodeciman bias.)

Eusebius. *The History of the Church From Christ to Constantine.*

HISTORY OF ANTI-SEMITISM

Gade, Richard E. *A Historical Survey of Anti-Semitism.*

HISTORY OF EASTER TRADITIONS AND CUSTOMS

Watts, Alan W. *Easter: Its Story and Meaning.*

Weiser, Francis X. *The Easter Book.*

Lord, Priscilla Sawyer and Foley, Daniel J. *Easter Garland.*

JUDAISM

Donin, Hayim Halevy. *To Be a Jew.*

Eckstein, Yechiel. *What Christians Should Know About Jews and Judaism.* (Written especially for Christians by a Jewish rabbi.)

Goldberg, Louis. *Our Jewish Friends.*

MESSIANIC JEWISH BELIEF ABOUT PASSOVER

Rosen, Ceil and Moishe. *Christ in the Passover.*

HAGGADAHS

Haggadah Shel Pesach. Complimentary Edition...Maxwell House. (Traditional Haggadah of Rabbinical Judaism. Available in some grocery stores during Passover season.)

Lipson, Eric-Peter. *Passover Haggadah.* (Messianic Jewish Haggadah.)

Raphael, Chaim. *A Feast of History...* (A modern translation of the Haggadah is included in this book.)

INDEXES

SCRIPTURE REFERENCES INDEX

GENERAL INDEX